To Frank, Sue, and Nan . . .
the nuts don't fall far from the tree.

LUCY GERSPACHER

Special Thanks
to the Hazelnut Marketing Board
for their support and assistance.

For a list of sources of
Oregon Hazelnut products, contact

Oregon Hazelnut Marketing Board
P.O. Box 23126
Portland, Oregon 97281
503/639-3118

International Standard Book Number 1-55868-203-1
Library of Congress Catalog Number 95-75449
Photographs © MCMXCV by the Hazelnut Marketing Board
Illustrations © MCMXCV by Graphic Arts Center Publishing™
Text © MCMXCV by Lucy Gerspacher
Food Styling • Lucy Gerspacher
Hazelnut Illustrations • Karen Hart
All rights reserved. No part of this book
may be copied without permission of the publisher.
Published by Graphic Arts Center Publishing™
P.O. Box 10306 • Portland, Oregon • 503/226-2402
President • Charles M. Hopkins
Editor-in-Chief • Douglas A. Pfeiffer
Managing Editor • Jean Andrews
Photo Editor • Diana S. Eilers
Production Manager • Richard L. Owsiany
Book Manufacturing • Lincoln & Allen Co.
Printed in the United States of America

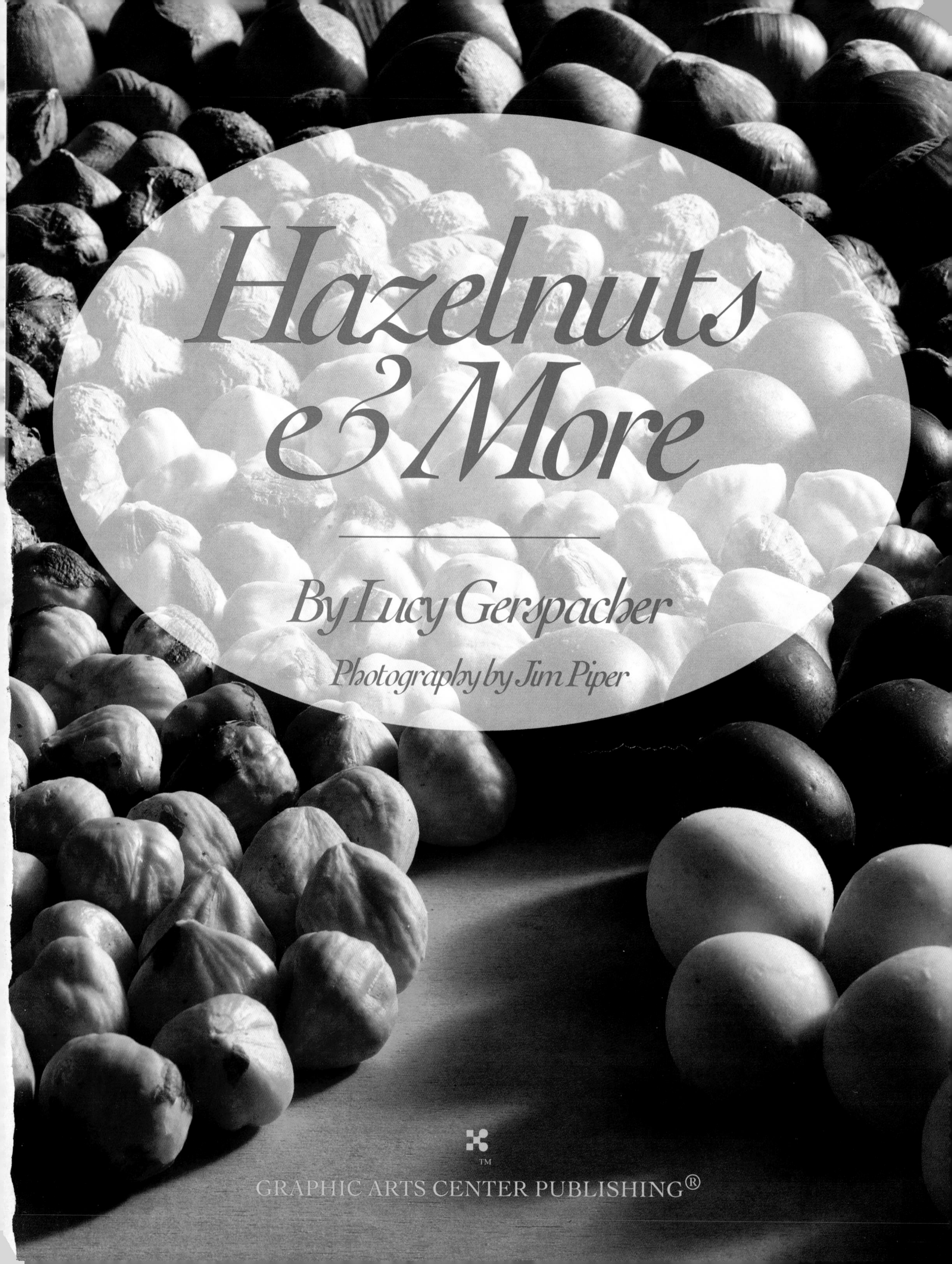

Hazelnuts & More

By Lucy Gerspacher

Photography by Jim Piper

GRAPHIC ARTS CENTER PUBLISHING®

Contents

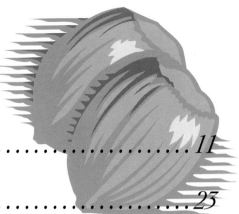

Ease of Preparation Key

◐   Easy for the average cook
◐ ◐   Still easy, but more steps
◐ ◐ ◐   Probably should know your way around in the kitchen
◐ ◐ ◐ ◐ Not for the timid

Mrs. DuChilly's Macaroons

By Lucy Gerspacher

DuChilly Macaroons

½ cup Eagle® Brand
     sweetened condensed milk
½ cup sliced (or chopped) filberts
2 cups shredded coconut

◐

Mix and drop by spoonfuls on a greased baking sheet, about one inch apart. Top each with a whole filbert. Bake in a moderate oven (350 degrees) for ten minutes or until a delicate brown. Remove from the pan at once.

This recipe holds special significance for me.

Several years ago, actually after I had been working with the Oregon Hazelnut Marketing Board for quite some time, Karen Lobb, the Promotions Manager for the Board, and I were asked to make a presentation about hazelnuts in history for the Oregon Historical Society.

I had a great time researching hazelnuts in early Oregon cooking. I found some very entertaining anecdotes from my Grandmother's turn-of-the-century cookbook, and I selected the above recipe to make for the audience. I thought the recipe was very appropriate as it had been a prize winner in a contest held by the Nut Growers Society in 1941. Also, I have a real weakness for anything with coconut, and this recipe was quick and easy to prepare.

Everything went along fine until, as we were tasting the cookies, someone asked me how the recipe got its name. Priding myself on my honesty with my students, and admitting it when I don't know an answer, I said that I really didn't know how the recipe got its name, but it was probably because a Mrs. DuChilly was the first one to make it.

At that point, Karen, in her quiet, polite way, said that perhaps the title was because DuChilly was a variety of hazelnuts.

Oops! Therein began my real education into the world of the hazelnut . . . and it has been delicious all the way.

I hope that you will enjoy this culinary adventure as we explore the many uses of this versatile nut. Oh yes, you can now ask me about the Barcelona, Ennis, Casina, *and* the DuChilly.

NOTE: Do try the above recipe. It is simple and delicious.

The Start of Something Big

The saga of a tiny seedling's rise from just a sprout in rural Oregon to star status as the State's official nut begins with the first tree planted in 1858 in Oregon's Umpqua Valley by an English sailor, Sam Strictland.

The tree grew and thrived.

About twenty years later, a Frenchman, David Gernot, sent to France for seeds of the thin-shell variety. Fifty trees produced from these seeds were planted in the Willamette Valley along a fence row, as was the practice in the Old Contry. There they thrived with little attention, providing food for the family and surrounding wildlife.

It was not until around 1885, however, that Felix Gillet, a resolute French horticulturist, introduced the Barcelona variety that is extensively grown today. And as they say, the rest is history.

Farmers started planting orchards. With a short growth time of only six years to commercial production and a productive life of up to forty years, hazelnuts became a viable crop in the state.

Today, Oregon produces between 98 and 99 percent of the total U.S. hazelnut crop. The cool summers, gentle winters, rainfall, and rich soil produce hazelnuts that are prized worldwide for their large size and quality.

Perhaps as testimony to those tenacious pioneers, that first tree planted in the Umpqua Valley of Oregon is still standing.

What's in a Name?

Let me introduce you to the hazelnut. You may have met before. I'm sure you recognize the smooth, round shell and the plump, sweet kernel, but I'll bet you met some time ago when this nut went by the name Filbert.

"Filbert" is thought by some historians to have originated from the Old English name, "full beard," because of the long husk that entirely covers the nut in some varieties. Others thought the name was derived from St. Philibert; August 22, the day dedicated to him, corresponds to the time, in England, of the ripening of the earliest filberts.

As children, we called the wild bushes that grew along fence rows and produced tiny nuts, hazelnuts. Their domesticated city cousins—which were pruned, pampered, and prized for the large nuts they produced—were called filberts.

When Oregon growers first started talking to the international market about exporting filberts, European chefs thought this must be some new strain of nut, not the hazelnuts they were accustomed to using in their fine pastries and confections.

At different times, this nut has been called the Cobb, the Cobb Nut, the Spanish Nut, the Pontic Nut, and the Lombard. No wonder there is confusion.

So now, to be consistent on the world market, we are referring to this premier nut, the pride of Oregon's lush Willamette Valley, as the hazelnut.

By any other name, it is still just as sweet and delicious.

Hazelnuts in History

No matter what the label, this nut has been around for a long time.

According to a manuscript found in China from the year 2838 B.C., the hazelnut took its place among the five sacred nourishments God bestowed on human beings. This tells us that hazelnuts, in some form, have been around for over 4500 years.

About 1800 years ago, the Greek physician, Dioscorides, thought he had a cure for baldness. His ointment—a mixture of burnt hazelnut shells and suet— was smeared on balding heads in the hope that the wily strands of hair would reappear.

A miracle cure? Maybe not—but I'll bet the resultant fragrance discouraged much ancient pillow talk.

He also thought that filberts, mixed with black pepper, cured the common cold. Ah yes, if only his cure had worked, he would have been a wealthy man. The good doctor also treated nagging coughs with a mixture of pounded hazelnuts and honey. Although the curative powers of this combination aren't proven, the sweet taste at least diverted attention from the ailing throat.

Many other ancient writings extol the curative properties of the hazelnut, or filbert. Mashed filberts and figs or raisins were used as a paste on the bite of a scorpion to take away the pain. Filbert leaves, boiled in water, were thought to be a blood purifier. The light coal produced by burning filbert wood was powdered and eaten as a cure for stomach problems.

While most of these remedies may seem futile by modern standards, the ancients were on the right track. Hazelnuts are nutritious. They are high in fiber and in minerals and vitamins such as calcium, potassium, magnesium, and Vitamin E. They are also a good source of protein and monounsaturated fats.

And they taste good too!

Storage, Equivalents, & Definitions

Storage:

The best place to store shelled hazelnuts is in the freezer at 27 degrees or less. They will last up to two years if stored in plastic bags or containers.

The next best place to store shelled hazelnuts is in the refrigerator at 32 to 35 degrees. They last up to one year if packaged in air-tight plastic bags or containers so they do not pick up odors. Before using, let nuts warm to room temperature in unopened bag.

Equivalents:

1 pound in-shell hazelnuts = 1½ cups hazelnut kernels
1 pound hazelnut kernels = 3¼ cups
1 cup hazelnut kernels = 1⅛ cups coarsely chopped
1 cup hazelnut kernels = 1¼ cups, finely chopped
1 cup hazelnut kernels = 1⅓ cups ground

Definitions:

Hazelnut Meal: Very finely ground hazelnuts used in commercial preparations as a binding agent or flour.

Finely ground toasted hazelnuts:
Hazelnuts that are ground in the food processor until they are very fine, but not yet butter.

Finely chopped toasted hazelnuts:
Hazelnuts that are chopped with a knife a little more coarsely than finely ground.

Medium chopped toasted hazelnuts:
Hazelnuts that are chopped with a knife into $1/16$ to $3/8$ inch pieces.

Coarsely chopped toasted hazelnuts:
Hazelnuts that are chopped with a knife into $1/4$ inch or larger pieces.

Roasting

Hazelnuts are delicious eaten right out of the shell. They have a sweet taste and a creamy texture. But they really shine when they are toasted (roasted). The flavor then turns smoky and robust and the texture is crisp and crunchy.

To toast hazelnuts, I prefer slow roasting in a preheated 275-degree oven. Spread shelled nuts in a shallow baking pan and roast at 275 degrees for 20 to 30 minutes, until the skins crack and the meat turns light golden.

Hazelnuts may also be roasted at higher temperatures. At 350 degrees, they will toast in only eight to ten minutes, but watch them closely, as they can go from toasted to scorched in a very short time at this temperature. If using a microwave, roast nuts at full power for three to four minutes.

To remove the skins, pour the hot nuts in the center of a rough kitchen terry towel. Pull the towel up around the nuts and twist tightly, making a hobo pack. Let stand to steam for about five minutes. Vigorously rub the warm nuts in the towel until most of the skins are removed. Remove the nuts and shake the towel outside in the garden.

Don't be concerned if some of the skins tenaciously cling to the nut. This is their nature, and the light-dark colors give hazelnuts a distinctive look.

Acknowledgments

A task of this size is never accomplished without the help and support of many people. There is never enough room to list everyone, but my special thanks go to:

Karen Lobb at the Oregon Hazelnut Marketing Board, Bud Donald at Westnut, and the Nut Growers Society for providing background information. Also, thanks to the many hazelnut growers and others who offered recipes and suggestions.

My husband Frank, one of those rare persons who eats just about anything and offers criticism kindly. As a pinch hitting recipe tester, he taught me that when you say "salt" in a recipe and do not specify an amount, it's not his fault if he uses a tablespoon instead of a pinch.

My recipe testers, Darlene Anderson, Charlotte Scharf, and Mary Ann Stadeli, whose suggestions were invaluable.

Sharon Bamford, Carole Bloom, Sadie Hunt, Carmen Jones, David Machado, Susan Mahoney, Bonnie Stewart Mickelson, Betsy Oppenneer, Betty Shenberger, Mary Ann Stadeli, and Nancie Steiner for sharing their expertise and recipes.

Carl Greve on Two, Mikasa and The 60's Cafe for providing photo props. Special thanks to Betty Shenberger for her exquisite taste in helping select vessels for the photography.

Rod Purdy of Fitt's Seafood, my favorite fish monger … Mike Dieker, fly tier extraordinaire … Pat Gerspacher for finding Uncle Matt's pancake recipe … Darren Steiner for keeping my computer humming … my mother, Ceil Bentz, who at age 91 still keeps a watchful eye for new hazelnut recipes … a special person, Trude Rose, for her quiet encouragement.

Special thanks to Sharon Tyler Herbst, whose wonderful reference book, the *Food Lover's Companion*, Barrons, 1990, was always at my fingertips … and to the many members of the Iinternational Association of Culinary Professionals whose generous sharing of information made my work so much easier.

*E*veryone enjoys appetizers. They are fun to serve, delicious to eat, and present an opportunity to set the tone of a gathering.

From a simple salted nut served with champagne to a splashy "designer" presentation, hazelnuts offer an interesting flavor and texture to almost any hors d'oeuvre or first course.

The distinctive, slightly smokey flavor of roasted hazelnuts adds dimension to old favorites like dips, spreads, pâtes, tarts, stuffed eggs and mushrooms. Hazelnuts also add an unexpected surprise to ethnic dishes like our Mediterranean Torta and East-West Pillows.

Although many of the recipes cook well as both appetizers and for buffet service, it is best to serve only one or two appetizers before a meal, so as not to steal the thunder from the "main event."

Presentations can be as simple as the use of a beautiful plate, or as elaborate as the imagination of the hosts will allow. While the use of interesting props is fun, I like the food to stand on its own; if any garnish is used on the food itself, it should be an ingredient from the recipe, such as herbs or citrus.

Broiled Mussels with Saffron

Since they are aqua farmed as a crop, mussels can be obtained year-round in most localities, although the flesh is firmest during the cold winter months. If you want to eat them whole, try to get mussels that are about 2 inches long. Also, don't try to pull the beards out. They are firmly rooted and are much more easily snipped off with scissors.

2 to 3 pounds small, fresh mussels
• Water
½ cup finely chopped toasted hazelnuts

Under cold, running water, scrub the mussels with a firm brush. Remove the beards by snipping with scissors. Place about two inches of cold water in a four-quart kettle and bring to a boil. Add cleaned mussels, cover, and return to a boil. Reduce heat and steam until shells open, about five minutes, stirring several times so the mussels are evenly cooked. Remove from liquid and discard any mussels that do not open.

Preheat broiler. Place mussels on the broiler pan. Be sure the upper shell is open wide enough to expose the meat to the heat. Divide Saffron Sauce among the mussels, sprinkle with hazelnuts, and broil approximately three inches from the heat for about one minute or until nuts start to brown. Serve immediately.

Saffron Sauce
¼ teaspoon saffron threads
2 tablespoons mussel cooking liquid
¾ cup mayonnaise
2 tablespoons fresh lemon juice
2 teaspoons minced fresh tarragon
• Salt to taste
• Pepper to taste

In a small measuring cup, sprinkle saffron threads over mussel liquid. Let stand for at least ten minutes for saffron to soften. Stir well.

Combine the liquid with mayonnaise, lemon juice, and tarragon. Season with salt and pepper to taste.

PRESENTATION TIP: Fill a large tray with about one-half inch of rock salt (obtained at most grocery stores). Place the shells in the rock salt to stabilize and to help hold the heat. Garnish with lemon slices and tarragon sprigs.

EASE OF
PREPARATION: 1

PREPARATION TIME:
20 MINUTES

COOKING TIME:
6 MINUTES

YIELD:
20 TO 30 MUSSELS,
DEPENDING ON SIZE

FOR PHOTO:
SEE OPPOSITE PAGE

NOTE: Painstakingly picked by hand, saffron is the orange stigma harvested from a special crocus plant. Although it is very expensive, it is almost always used in very small quantities. The amount used in this recipe should cost less than $1.00. Saffron threads can be found at most well-stocked grocery stores or specialty food sections.

East-West Pillows

EASE OF
PREPARATION: 3

PREPARATION TIME
FILLING:
20 MINUTES

ASSEMBLY TIME:
20 MINUTES

BAKING TIME:
15 MINUTES

YIELD: 24

FOR PHOTO:
SEE PAGE 12

DID YOU KNOW...
That the hazelnut is
Oregon's "official
State Nut."

This filling is more likely to be found in a spring roll than in Greek pastry. Combining the Oriental filling with the traditional Greek Tiropete, or triangle, results in a delicious mingling of the two cultures.

½ cup coarsely chopped Pink Bay Shrimp
⅓ cup coarsely chopped toasted hazelnuts
⅓ cup finely chopped celery
⅓ cup grated carrot
2 tablespoons finely chopped green onion
2 tablespoons diced sweet red pepper
   (⅛ inch dice)
2 tablespoons chopped cilantro
1 tablespoon soy sauce
1 teaspoon sesame oil
¼ teaspoon finely crushed
   red pepper flakes
1 egg white
8 sheets Phyllo (Fillo) dough, unthawed
½ cup clarified butter
   (See Glossary, pages 123-124)

Heat oven to 400 degrees.

In a small bowl, mix together all ingredients up through and including red pepper flakes. Whisk egg white until frothy and stir into mixture. Set aside.

On a flat surface, lay out one full sheet of fillo and brush lightly with melted butter. Lay a second sheet on top and brush with melted butter. With a sharp knife or pizza cutter, cut sheet into six crosswise strips.

Spoon about two teaspoons of the filling in the bottom righthand corner of each strip, about one inch up from the bottom. Fold the left corner up and over the filling, making a diagonal fold. Continue folding, flagstyle, until all of the strip is folded into a multilayered triangle. Brush with melted butter and repeat with the remaining strips, continuing until all of the filling is used.

The pastries may be frozen at this point and baked frozen, or they may be refrigerated for several hours. Just make sure they are tightly covered. Bake in a 400-degree oven for about 15 minutes, or until golden brown. Add several minutes to baking time if frozen.

About Phyllo (Fillo) dough:

Phyllo dough is the tissue-thin dough used to make a delicate, many-layered pastry. In larger cities, fresh Phyllo dough is available from Greek markets, although it is most often used in frozen form, purchased at supermarkets.

The frozen dough should be allowed to thaw in the refrigerator, preferably overnight. Completely defrost dough before using, or the sheets will tear.

In order to obtain the crispy layered texture, each layer is brushed with butter to ensure that the layers separate when baking. Although butter is usually used, if desired, olive oil may be used in place of butter to separate the layers, but the pastry will not brown as well when oil is used. A final brushing over the top with clarified butter will expedite browning.

When working with the pastry sheets, care should be taken that they do not become too damp (they will disintegrate), or dry out (they will get brittle). A kitchen towel that has been dampened and rung almost dry may be used to cover the sheets when not in use; however, if left on the dough too long it will start to soften. A piece of wide plastic wrap under the towel may solve this problem.

Sheets that tear are always difficult to work with, but they can be easily pieced together with a little butter; when they are on the inside layers, it makes little difference in the finished product. However, try to have an untorn sheet for the bottom and top.

NOTE: Cover any leftover Phyllo sheets with a piece of plastic wrap and tightly reroll. Seal in the original plastic container, if possible and refrigerate for up to two weeks.

NOTE: On the West Coast, the small, cooked, ready-to-eat pink shrimp are known as Oregon Pink Shrimp. They may be called salad shrimp, pink shrimp, bay shrimp, or shrimp meat in other parts of the country.

Lime & Garlic Shrimp with Hazelnut Stuffing

⬭ ⬭

**EASE OF
PREPARATION: 2**

**PREPARATION TIME:
30 MINUTES**

**MARINATING TIME:
1 TO 2 HOURS**

**COOKING TIME:
2 TO 4 MINUTES**

**YIELD:
20 TO 30 SHRIMP**

**FOR PHOTO:
SEE PAGE 12**

NOTE: In large
shrimp it is
necessary to remove
the intestinal vein
which runs along
the back of the
shrimp. There is a
special tool called a
"Shrimp De-veiner,"
but simply running a
sharp knife down
beside the vein and
lifting it out works
just fine. Sometimes
the vein is removed
during processing
and further work is
unnecessary.

This is a special company dish, so buy the biggest shrimp your budget will allow. If the shrimp are extremely large, however, it may be necessary to cook them partially under the broiler before stuffing so the filling doesn't burn before the shrimp are thoroughly cooked.

1 pound large shrimp (prawns),
   20 to 30 count

Marinade
¼ cup fresh lime juice
2 tablespoons hazelnut or vegetable oil
2 cloves garlic, minced
1 tablespoon fresh chopped dill weed
   (1 teaspoon dried)

Stuffing
½ cup toasted bread crumbs
½ cup finely chopped roasted hazelnuts
¼ cup grated parmesan cheese
2 tablespoons melted butter
• Dash salt
• Freshly ground black pepper to taste

⬭

Peel shrimp, leaving the tails intact. De-vein if necessary. Slit shrimp on the underside, from head to tail, about half way through the meat, so they will lie flat.

In 1½ quart glass bowl, whisk together all ingredients for marinade. Place shrimp in marinade for one to two hours. Remove from marinade, drain and lay flat, cut side up on broiler pan. Heat broiler.

Combine all ingredients for stuffing. Place a teaspoon or two of stuffing on shrimp. Drizzle with remaining marinade. Broil three inches from the broiler, until stuffing is browned and shrimp turn pink, about two to four minutes, depending upon the size of the shrimp. Serve immediately.

NOTE: The amount of stuffing used will vary depending upon the size of the shrimp. The stuffing recipe may be doubled or tripled.

PRESENTATION TIP: Serve in a large baking shell, or place several on smaller baking shells arranged on a large tray. Garnish with lime slices and fresh dill weed.

Savory Roasted Hazelnuts

This is the basic recipe for seasoned, roasted hazelnuts. Different flavors can be created by adding ingredients such as Worcestershire sauce, hot pepper sauce, garlic powder, onion powder, chile seasoning, dill weed, herbs, curry, or any other desired flavors.

2 tablespoons butter
2 tablespoons vegetable oil
4 cups shelled, raw hazelnuts
• Salt to taste

Heat oven to 275 degrees.

Combine butter and oil in a 10 x 15 x 1 inch baking sheet. Place in a warm oven for several minutes until butter is melted. Add hazelnuts and stir so that all the nuts are coated with the butter and oil mixture.

Bake in a 275-degree oven until nuts are golden, about 20 minutes. Remove from oven and sprinkle with salt or any other desired flavoring. Toss to evenly distribute seasoning. Cool and serve.

NOTE: Store the nuts in a tightly covered container for up to two weeks. Store in freezer for up to two months.

EASE OF
PREPARATION: 1

PREPARATION TIME:
5 MINUTES

BAKING TIME:
20 MINUTES

YIELD: 4 CUPS

Baked Brie with Hazelnuts & Mangoes

If fresh mango is unavailable, mango chutney can be used for an interesting substitute. Whole cranberry sauce is also a nice variation.

1 8-ounce round brie cheese
⅔ cup coarsely chopped, toasted hazelnuts
¼ cup brown sugar, divided
1 ripe mango (¾ cup chopped)
1 tablespoon fresh lemon juice
¼ teaspoon curry powder

Heat oven to 350 degrees.

With a sharp knife, slice rind off top of cheese. Cut round in half horizontally. Sprinkle the cut surface of the bottom half with one tablespoon brown sugar. Press ⅓ cup of the hazelnuts into the brown sugar. Replace the top half; press together firmly.

Sprinkle the top with another tablespoon of brown sugar, and press the remaining hazelnuts into the surface.

Peel the mango and cut into ¼-inch chunks. Place in a small bowl and mix with lemon juice, the remaining two tablespoons brown sugar, and the curry powder.

Place brie on a shallow baking sheet and bake in a 350-degree oven for about five minutes. Spoon mango over the top and continue baking for another three minutes.

Serve hot with crusty French bread slices.

EASE OF
PREPARATION: 1

PREPARATION TIME:
10 MINUTES

BAKING TIME:
8 MINUTES

YIELD:
SERVES 4

Hazelnut-Cheddar Biscuits with Smoked Salmon-Artichoke Filling

EASE OF
PREPARATION: 1

PREPARATION TIME:
15 MINUTES

BAKING TIME:
12 MINUTES

YIELD:
36 1-INCH BISCUITS

NOTE: The use of
cake flour makes the
biscuits extra light.

These biscuits, with just a hint of hazelnuts, are delicious with any number of fillings. They are also good served split with butter as an accompaniment to soups and salads. They will keep for several weeks in the freezer.

1 cup all purpose flour
1 cup cake flour
2 teaspoons baking powder
½ teaspoon salt
¼ cup (½ stick) cold butter
1 cup (4 ounces) grated medium
   cheddar cheese
¼ cup finely chopped toasted hazelnuts
2 tablespoons chopped fresh chives
¾ cup milk

Position baking rack in the upper ⅓ of the oven and heat the oven to 425 degrees.

In a large bowl sift together all purpose flour, cake flour, baking powder, and salt. With pastry blender or fingertips, mix butter into dry ingredients until it is roughly pea sized. Mix in cheddar cheese, hazelnuts, and chives. Add milk, and mix until ingredients are just moistened.

Turn dough out onto a lightly floured surface and knead several times. Pat into a circle about ¾ inch thick. Cut into rounds with a floured one-inch biscuit cutter. Place on an ungreased cookie sheet and bake in the upper third of a 425-degree oven until golden, about twelve minutes.

Cool on rack. Split and serve with Smoked Salmon-Artichoke Filling.

Smoked Salmon-Artichoke Filling

4 ounces smoked salmon
¼ cup drained, coarsely chopped
   marinated artichokes
2 tablespoons chopped green onions
1 tablespoon drained, small capers
   (See Glossary, pages 123-124)
1 tablespoon fresh lemon juice
• Mayonnaise
• Freshly ground black pepper to taste

Remove bones and skin from smoked salmon and flake into small pieces. Mix with remaining ingredients, moistening with just enough mayonnaise to hold it together. Refrigerate.

My thanks to Sadie Hunt who developed this colorful appetizer. She sometimes adds roasted red peppers, which add a rich, smokey flavor.

1 5½-ounce package chèvre
   (soft goat cheese), room temperature
4 ounces cream cheese, room temperature
1 cup coarsely chopped toasted hazelnuts
1 cup oil packed, sun dried tomatoes,
   drained (about 6 ounces)
1 bunch fresh basil, washed and dried

In small bowl mix goat cheese and cream cheese together until well blended. Fold in hazelnuts. Set aside.

For a mold, line a two-cup round, plastic refrigerator dish with plastic wrap, extending it over the sides by about two inches.

Pat the sun dried tomatoes dry with paper towels. Place tomatoes in a single layer to cover the bottom of the mold. Spread one-fourth of the cheese mixture on top of tomatoes. With the back of a spoon, pack cheese firmly into the mold.

Place whole basil leaves in a single layer on top of cheese. Continue layering to form four layers of the three ingredients, until all are used.

Pull extended plastic over the top of the mold, and refrigerate for at least two hours, or until firm.

Mediterranean Torta

Unmold onto serving dish. Garnish with additional basil leaves and nuts. Serve with crackers or toasted bread slices.

Toasted Bread Slices

Slice baguettes in ½-inch slices. Lightly brush tops with butter and bake in a 350-degree oven until light brown, about 15 minutes. Cool.

NOTE: Be sure to pack the ingredients down after each addition, as this is what "glues" the mold together.

NOTE: Goat cheese is a fairly moist white cheese that most often comes in a log or rounds, sometimes marinated in a flavored oil or seasoned with herbs or pepper. It has a distinctive flavor that blends well with highly flavored foods. Plain or marinated cheese works well.

EASE OF
PREPARATION: 2

PREPARATION TIME:
10 MINUTES

CHILLING TIME:
2 HOURS

YIELD:
SERVES 6 TO 8 FOR
APPETIZERS

DID YOU KNOW...
That hazelnuts are higher in Vitamin E and have more monounsaturated fatty acids than other nuts.

Hazelnut, Bacon & Apple Stuffed Mushrooms

EASE OF
PREPARATION: 1

PREPARATION TIME:
20 MINUTES

BAKING TIME:
5 MINUTES

YIELD:
20 MUSHROOMS

Stuffed mushrooms are an old favorite that deserve a revival. This combination of bacon, apples, and nuts is always a hit. Be sure not to overbake the mushrooms, as they will shrink and become watery.

20 Button or Brown Crimini mushrooms,
    about 1½ inches in diameter
3 slices thick sliced bacon
½ cup finely chopped onion
¼ teaspoon salt
• Freshly ground black pepper to taste
½ cup coarsely chopped tart apple
    (Granny Smith, McIntosh, etc.)
½ cup fresh bread crumbs
½ cup coarsely chopped toasted hazelnuts
½ cup grated parmesan cheese

Heat oven to 425 degrees.

Wash and dry mushrooms. Carefully remove the stems without breaking the caps. Reserve caps. With food processor fitted with metal blade or by hand, finely chop the stems. Set aside.

In a large skillet, fry the bacon until crisp. Drain on paper towels. Crumble into small pieces.

Pour off all but two tablespoons of the bacon drippings. Over medium-high heat, sauté onion in bacon drippings until softened, about three minutes. Add chopped mushroom stems and sauté until most of the moisture has evaporated, about five minutes, stirring often. Season with salt and pepper to taste. Add remaining ingredients, along with reserved crumbled bacon, and toss until well mixed.*

Stuff the reserved mushroom caps with the mixture, mounding it slightly on the top. Place on ungreased baking sheet and bake in a 425-degree oven until heated through, about five minutes.

Serve immediately.

* If the mixture is too dry to hold together, add a tablespoon of dry, white wine or Chicken Stock (page 37) to help bind it.

TO SELECT, CLEAN & STORE MUSHROOMS:
Select mushrooms that are firm and heavy for their size, with very few gills showing on the underside. Avoid any that are soft, broken or damaged. Mushrooms should be used as soon as possible after purchase and should not be cleaned until just before using. To clean mushrooms, place a comfortable amount in your cupped hands. Hold them under cold, running water while gently rubbing. Pat dry with terry towel, rubbing off any soil that remains. Store mushrooms in the refrigerator in a container where air can circulate, covered with a paper towel, or in a brown bag. Do not store in plastic bags.

Sweet & Sour Hazelnut Drumettes

The flat part of the chicken wings can also be used in this recipe; however, because they are quite fatty and difficult to eat with one hand, I prefer to keep them for other uses, such as in stock.

½ cup apricot jam

¼ cup port wine

1 tablespoon vinegar

2 teaspoons dijon mustard

1 teaspoon minced fresh ginger

1 clove garlic, minced

¼ teaspoon red pepper flakes

1 teaspoon cornstarch

1 tablespoon cold water

12 drumstick portions of chicken wings

• Flour for dredging

2 tablespoons vegetable oil

• Salt to taste

• Pepper to taste

¼ cup finely chopped toasted hazelnuts

In a small saucepan, combine apricot jam, port wine, vinegar, mustard, ginger, garlic, and red pepper flakes. Bring to a boil, reduce heat, and simmer for about ten minutes. Strain, return liquid to the pan, and discard solids.

Dissolve cornstarch in cold water. Whisk into sauce and cook for several minutes over medium heat until sauce thickens. Set aside.

In the meantime, prepare chicken. Trim away any excess fat. Remove skin, if desired. Using a sharp knife, on the smaller end of the drumette, cut the skin and tendons in a circle around the bone. Using the same knife, scrape the meat toward the meatier end. With fingers, pull the meat up and over the joint, forming a knob or ball. Dredge in flour.

Heat oven to 400 degrees.

Heat oil in large skillet and brown chicken on both sides, about five minutes per side. Season with salt and pepper. Spray a shallow baking dish with nonstick vegetable spray, and arrange chicken in the dish.

Brush with sauce and bake in a 400-degree oven for 20 minutes, turning, basting, and sprinkling with hazelnuts several times. Let stand for about five minutes before serving.

Can be frozen. Reheat on baking sheet in a 400-degree oven.

EASE OF
PREPARATION: 2

PREPARATION TIME:
30 MINUTES

BAKING TIME:
20 MINUTES

YIELD:
12 APPETIZERS

PRESENTATION TIP:
Arrange in a circle, on a large round plate or tray, with the bone end pointing to the edge of the plate. A small dish of coarsely chopped hazelnuts may be placed in the center for additional dipping.

Smoked Salmon Pâté

If smoked salmon is unavailable, use cooked fresh salmon and a little liquid smoke to taste, about ¼ teaspoon.

1 small clove garlic
1 small shallot
2 tablespoons parsley leaves
1 teaspoon fresh thyme leaves
    (½ teaspoon dried)
6 oz. smoked salmon
8 ounces cream cheese, room temperature
2 tablespoons sour cream
1 tablespoon fresh lemon juice
¼ teaspoon salt
• Dash freshly ground black pepper
½ cup finely chopped toasted hazelnuts

Place garlic, shallot, parsley and thyme in a food processor fitted with a metal blade. Process until very fine, about 20 seconds.

Remove skin and bones from the salmon, add to work bowl, and chop fine, about ten seconds. Add cream cheese and process until smooth, about ten seconds. Mix in sour cream, lemon juice, salt and pepper to taste. Fold in hazelnuts.

Serve with thin slices of black bread or crackers.

PRESENTATION TIP: Spread pâté on a serving platter in the shape of a fish, and chill for a minimum of one hour, or up to overnight. Garnish with thinly sliced cucumber for scales, a slice of olive for the eye, red pepper or radish for the mouth, and red pepper for gills.

Garnish
1 small cucumber
1 green olive
• red pepper slices

Savory Hazelnut Cocktail Wafers

Although they may look like cookies, these savory little wafers surprise the palate with a savory, slightly peppery bite. Excellent served with wine or champagne.

1½ cups finely ground,
    toasted hazelnuts, divided
1 cup all-purpose white flour
1 cup finely ground parmesan cheese
¼ teaspoon salt
¼ teaspoon (or more) hot pepper sauce
½ cup butter, room temperature,
    cut in ½-inch pieces
2 tablespoons water

In a food processor fitted with metal blade, combine ½ cup ground hazelnuts, flour, parmesan, salt, and hot pepper sauce. Process until well mixed, about ten seconds.

Add butter and process for an additional fifteen seconds, or until butter is finely chopped. With the machine running, add water; process until dough sticks together, about ten seconds.

Remove dough from work bowl and divide into four equal parts. On plastic wrap, roll each piece into a log 1¼ inches in diameter and about 10 to 12 inches long. Roll in remaining hazelnuts. Wrap tightly in plastic wrap and chill until firm, about 10 minutes in freezer, or 30 minutes in refrigerator.

Shortly before baking, position an oven rack in the center of the oven and heat oven to 375 degrees. Slice chilled rolls into ¼-inch-thick rounds. Place on ungreased baking sheet, one inch apart, and bake until golden, about 12 to 15 minutes. Remove from the pan and cool on racks.

Whether they are used as an ingredient or as a garnish, toasted hazelnuts can give salads an interesting dimension. Especially in winter, when the quality of fresh vegetables hits a low—and the price hits a high—just a touch of hazelnuts can add pizzaz to an otherwise ordinary salad.

Hazelnut oil also adds a subtle, nutty flavor, especially when used with citrus salads or with mild, fruity vinegars. A small amount of hazelnut oil combined with a lighter oil gives salads a subtle essence of hazelnuts.

Of the many types of vinegar on the market, one of the mildest is Oriental Rice Vinegar. Balsamic vinegar, from Italy, also has a mild, sweet flavor and a distinctive, mellow quality from long aging in wooden barrels. Herb, wine, and fruit vinegars range from sweet to very tart, depending on the manufacturer. Because vinegars vary so much in strength, it is necessary to taste and adjust the ingredients when preparing the dressing.

The amount of fat in a vinaigrette may be reduced by partially replacing the oil with fruit juices, wine, or champagne. Adding a small amount of sugar or honey to the dressing will also help lessen the bite of a tart vinegar, and therefore less oil will be needed for flavor balance.

Toss salads with just enough dressing to give flavor and moisture to the ingredients, without oversaturating. In some of the following recipes, there may be dressing left over because—especially in pasta and rice salads—the ingredients will absorb differing amounts of dressing, depending on their density. Pasta and rice are notorious for absorbing liquids, and sometimes salads made with these ingredients taste flat. Adding only half of the dressing before chilling and the rest just before serving assures a flavorful salad.

I prefer to use a food processor or mini-chop to make vinaigrette because both of these machines blend the ingredients so well that the solids are held in suspension for quite a long period of time, thereby making a nice creamy dressing.

Salad making is where creativity reigns supreme. In most of the following recipes, it doesn't hurt to deviate a bit from the original formula. If you don't like an ingredient like Greek olives, leave them out. But do try the recipe with your own favorite substitution. And remember, hazelnuts make just about any salad taste better!

Smoked Salmon, Artichoke & Wild Rice Salad with Hazelnuts

This salad holds well and looks great for buffet service. A cold glass of Chardonnay makes a wonderful accompaniment. Be sure to reserve a little of the dressing to refresh the salad, as the brown rice tends to absorb a lot of liquid.

3 cups cooked brown rice,
   drained and chilled
1 cup cooked wild rice, drained and chilled
   (See page 61)
1 cup boned and flaked smoked salmon
1 6-ounce jar marinated artichoke hearts,
   drained and sliced in quarters (1 cup)
½ cup green onions,
   sliced diagonally in 1-inch pieces
2 tablespoons chopped parsley
2 tablespoons chopped fresh dillweed
   (2 teaspoons dried)
½ cup coarsely chopped toasted hazelnuts

In a large bowl, combine all ingredients except hazelnuts. Add half of the dressing to the salad ingredients. Chill for several hours. Just before serving, add remaining dressing. Mix in hazelnuts.

Dressing

1 clove garlic, peeled
1 small shallot, peeled
1 tablespoon fresh tarragon leaves
   (1 teaspoon dried)
1 tablespoon fresh dillweed leaves
   (1 teaspoon dried)
½ cup light vegetable oil
⅓ cup fresh lemon juice
1 tablespoon honey
1 teaspoon dijon mustard
¼ teaspoon salt
• Freshly ground black pepper to taste

Mince garlic and shallot by pulsing several times in a food processor or mini-chop. Add remaining ingredients and process until smooth and creamy. Adjust seasonings to taste.

Garnish with lemon slices, fresh dill, and cucumber slices.

EASE OF
PREPARATION: 2

PREPARATION TIME:
20 MINUTES

COOKING TIME:
45 MINUTES TO
COOK RICE

CHILLING TIME:
2 HOURS

YIELD:
6 TO 8 SERVINGS

PHOTO:
OPPOSITE PAGE

PRESENTATION TIP:
This looks beautiful when served on a clear glass plate, preferably a fish plate if you have one. Mound the salad on the plate, top with several lemon slices and a sprig of fresh dill. Surround with a swirl of cucumber slices.

Salad of Fresh Pear, Greens, & Honeyed Hazelnuts

EASE OF
PREPARATION: 2

PREPARATION TIME:
15 MINUTES

YIELD: 6 SERVINGS

PHOTO: INCLUDED
IN COVER IMAGE

DID YOU KNOW...
That in-shell
hazelnuts are called
just that: in-shell
nuts. Shelled nuts
are known as
kernels.

Pear and bleu cheese is a classic flavor combination. Add honeyed hazelnuts for an unbeatable threesome.

Salad
6 cups mixed greens*
2 ripe pears, cored and sliced
    (Bartlett, Red Bartlett, Comice, etc.)
• Fresh lemon juice
½ cup crumbled bleu cheese
1 cup Honeyed Hazelnuts

Rub the cut edges of the pear with lemon juice. Divide the greens among six serving plates. Top with pear slices and bleu cheese. Drizzle with Pear Vinaigrette and sprinkle with Honeyed Hazelnuts.

NOTE: If using a beautiful pear like a Red Bartlett, the peeling may be left on. If using a less attractive fruit, it is best to peel before using.

* NOTE: To crisp greens, see Cajun Scallop Salad, page 28.

Pear Vinaigrette
2 ripe pear halves
1 tablespoon lemon juice
2 tablespoons white vinegar
2 tablespoons hazelnut oil
    (See Glossary, pages 123-124)
    or light vegetable oil
1 tablespoon honey
1 teaspoon lemon zest
    (See Glossary, pages 123-124)

In food processor fitted with metal blade, chop pears with lemon juice. Add remaining ingredients and process until smooth, 30 to 60 seconds.

Honeyed Hazelnuts
2 tablespoons butter
¼ cup honey
1 cup whole toasted hazelnuts

In a small sauce pan, melt butter over medium heat. Add honey and cook until mixture turns a deep caramel color. Add nuts, stir to coat, and pour out onto parchment paper. Separate nuts with a fork and cool. Store in an air-tight container.

NOTE: For the dressing, the pear halves should be soft enough to easily pierce with a fork. If they are not, poach in a light syrup (1 cup water and ½ cup sugar) until they are softened. Canned pears may also be used.

Fresh Fruit Salad with Hazelnut Lemon Sauce

This refreshing summer fruit bowl can be served either as a salad or as a dessert. The Hazelnut Praline adds an interesting texture and flavor as the moisture from the dressing melts the candy coating on the nuts.

4 to 6 cups fresh seasonal fruit (melons, berries, peaches, nectarines, etc.)
• Hazelnut Lemon Sauce

Prepare fruit by washing and cutting in serving-sized pieces. Arrange in platter or serving bowl. Serve the Hazelnut Lemon Sauce on the side.

Hazelnut Lemon Sauce
½ cup whipping cream
1 8-ounce cup lemon yogurt
1 tablespoon honey
1 tablespoon orange liqueur
   (such as Grand Marnier)

In a small bowl, whip cream until soft peaks form. In another bowl, whisk together lemon yogurt, honey, and orange liqueur. Fold in whipped cream. Just before serving, mix in ¼ cup Hazelnut Praline.

Hazelnut Praline
½ cup granulated sugar
⅓ cup orange juice
½ cup finely chopped toasted hazelnuts

Place sugar and orange juice in a one-quart saucepan and swirl to dissolve sugar. Boil until the mixture turns a medium caramel color, about five minutes. Stir in nuts and rapidly pour out onto a buttered baking sheet. With a knife, spread as thin as possible. The mixture will harden as it cools. When cool, break into ¼ inch pieces, or place in food processor and chop.

EASE OF PREPARATION: 2

PREPARATION TIME:
15 MINUTES,
DEPENDING UPON
CHOICE OF FRUIT

COOKING TIME:
5 MINUTES

YIELD:
6 TO 8 SERVINGS

PHOTO: PAGE 6

NOTE: May use orange juice concentrate in place of liqueur.

DID YOU KNOW...
That 99% of the nation's commercial hazelnut crop comes from Oregon.

Cajun Scallop Salad

EASE OF
PREPARATION: 2

PREPARATION TIME:
15 MINUTES

COOKING TIME:
5 MINUTES

YIELD: 4 SERVINGS

NOTE: To crisp
greens, with a sharp
knife cut off a thin
slice of the stem end
of the head of
lettuce. Immerse in
tepid water for about
1 hour. Pull the
leaves apart and
wrap in a clean terry
towel. Refrigerate
for several hours
until crisp.

Be sure to use the large sea scallops, as the smaller bay scallops are just too easy to overcook with the high heat necessary for quick browning.

If you like, you can use the bacon drippings as part of the oil for the dressing. It is delicious, but also laden with cholesterol.

Salad
4 cups (approximate) chopped
    mixed greens
1 medium ripe tomato, cut in wedges
1 medium cucumber, thinly sliced
½ green pepper, thinly sliced
4 green onions, thinly sliced
• Alfalfa sprouts
1 pound sea scallops
• Vegetable oil
½ teaspoon Cajun spices
¾ cup coarsely chopped toasted hazelnuts
• Freshly ground black pepper to taste

Divide greens, tomato, cucumber, green pepper, and green onion among four plates. Make a little nest in the center with alfalfa sprouts.

Heat skillet until very hot. Toss scallops with just enough vegetable oil to lightly coat. Sprinkle with Cajun spices; press into the scallops. Very quickly cook the scallops, about one to two minutes per side, so that they are dark on the outside and moist in the center.

To serve, place the scallops in the sprout nests, dividing evenly among the four plates. Drizzle dressing over the salads, sprinkle with chopped hazelnuts and freshly ground black pepper. Serve immediately.

Dressing
4 pieces thick-sliced bacon
½ cup vegetable oil
¼ cup balsamic vinegar
2 tablespoons dry red wine
2 tablespoons honey
1 teaspoon dry mustard
1 teaspoon Cajun spices
½ teaspoon minced fresh ginger
1 egg yolk
2 tablespoons minced parsley

In a medium skillet, fry bacon until crisp. Drain on paper towels and crumble when cool. Pour bacon drippings into a metal container. Reserve for another use.

In the same skillet, heat oil, vinegar, wine, honey, mustard, Cajun spices, and ginger until simmering. Remove from heat for several minutes and quickly whisk in egg yolk. Return to low heat, stirring constantly, until mixture thickens slightly and temperature reaches 160 degrees. (See Eggs, Glossary, pages 123-124) Remove from heat immediately.

Just before serving, add parsley and reserved bacon.

NOTE: Cajun spices can be purchased at most well-stocked grocery stores or specialty food markets.

Thai Chicken Salad

This low-fat dinner salad was developed by my daughter, Nancie Steiner. She has used an interesting combination of flavors in the dressing to replace the oil customarily required.

Grill chicken breasts while preparing the rest of the salad, or if your prefer, they may be grilled ahead of time and reheated in the microwave.

Salad

2 grilled boneless and skinless
   chicken breasts, diagonally sliced
4 cups tossed mixed greens*
2 cups thinly sliced cabbage
1 medium carrot, thinly sliced
1 medium cucumber, thinly sliced
1 cup crispy Chinese noodles
4 tablespoons chopped toasted hazelnuts

Divide mixed greens, cabbage, carrot and cucumber among four plates. Top with a bed of crispy noodles and several slices of chicken. Drizzle dressing over greens and chicken. Sprinkle with hazelnuts and serve.

* To crisp greens, see Cajun Scallop Salad, page 28.

Thai Dressing

1 clove garlic, minced
1 1-inch chunk ginger, peeled and minced
¼ teaspoon red pepper flakes
¼ cup cilantro leaves
¼ cup soy sauce
¼ cup dry sherry
2 tablespoons vinegar
1 tablespoon lime juice
1 tablespoon honey
1 tablespoon sesame oil
¼ cup vegetable oil

In a food processor or mini-chop, finely mince garlic, ginger, red pepper and cilantro. Add remaining ingredients and blend well. (Add more hot peppers, if desired). Let stand for several hours for flavors to meld.

EASE OF
PREPARATION: 2

PREPARATION TIME:
15 MINUTES

GRILLING TIME:
10 MINUTES

YIELD:
4 LARGE SERVINGS

NOTE: If desired, 1½ tablespoons apple juice concentrate may be used in place of the honey.

NOTE: The dressing will keep for up to 2 weeks tightly covered in the refrigerator.

Smoked Chicken, Orange & Hazelnut Salad

EASE OF
PREPARATION: 1

PREPARATION TIME:
20 MINUTES

CHILLING TIME:
2 HOURS

YIELD:
8 SERVINGS

DID YOU KNOW...
That hazelnuts
were placed among
the five sacred
nourishments God
bestowed to
humans, according
to a Chinese
manuscript dated at
2838 B.C.

*This versatile salad can be made with smoked
turkey as well as chicken. If smoked chicken or
turkey is unavailable, try using plain cooked
poultry and add a dash of liquid smoke in the
dressing.*

4 cups cubed smoked chicken
1 orange, peeled and diced
1 cup red seedless grapes, halved
    (red flame variety)
2 stalks celery, thinly sliced
¼ cup thinly sliced green onions
½ cup coarsely chopped hazelnuts

Combine above ingredients, except
hazelnuts, in a large bowl. Toss with
Creamy Orange Dressing and chill for
several hours. Add hazelnuts just before
serving.

Creamy Orange Dressing
¾ cup mayonnaise
¼ cup plain yogurt
2 tablespoons raspberry vinegar
1 tablespoon orange juice concentrate
2 teaspoons orange zest
1 teaspoon minced fresh ginger
½ teaspoon curry powder
¼ teaspoon salt
• Dash freshly ground black pepper

Whisk all ingredients together until
smooth. If too thick to pour, add milk or
orange juice, one tablespoon at a time, until
desired consistency. Refrigerate.

Garnish with grapes, orange slices,
chopped hazelnuts, or mint leaves

PRESENTATION TIP: Mound salad in center
of round or oblong plate. Garnish with
additional chopped hazelnuts. Tuck orange
slices and mint leaves around the salad and
add several bunches of tiny grapes, if
available. The tiny, purple Champagne
grapes that are available in the summer
look especially nice as garnish.

Hazelnuts are sometimes an integral part of a soup recipe, as in Creamy Squash and Bacon Soup, or they may be used to tease the palate where not expected, as in Fresh Apple Soup with Hazelnut Apple Balls. Almost any cream or thickened soup will benefit from a sprinkling of toasted hazelnuts as a garnish.

There seems to be one widely accepted fallacy regarding soup making. That is, that soup only gets better the longer it is cooked. This is only partly true. Most stocks improve with long, slow cooking, but when making the actual soup, overcooking results in mushy vegetables, soggy pasta, and tough meat. The secret to success in soup making is often in the stock.

Home made stocks have a fresh, clean flavor that is difficult to find in commercially prepared products. They are not difficult to make, but they do need plenty of cooking time for complex flavors to develop. Long, slow cooking in an uncovered pot allows moisture to evaporate and intensifies the flavor of the stock.

Adding salt to stock is not generally recommended; however, I do like to add a small amount to bring out the flavors and make it easier to taste the strength of the broth. Apart from vegetable stock, which sometimes needs intense flavors to develop the base, most stocks should be seasoned lightly, so they are versatile enough to use in many different recipes. Because of variations in saltiness of stocks, most of the soup recipes call for "Salt to taste," rather than a specific amount.

The variety of herbs used for flavoring will differ with the type of the stock, but a Bouquet Garni (a little bouquet of herbs tied together or in cheesecloth) is somewhat easier to use than herbs added separately because it is easier to remove from the finished broth. Most stocks will keep for several days in the refrigerator, or for several months in the freezer.

Bouquet Garni
1 bay leaf
1 sprig fresh thyme
3 to 4 parsley stems
8 peppercorns

Tie in small square of cheesecloth.

NOTE: Most of our recipes make eight to ten cups of soup. We like leftovers!

The inspiration for this recipe was a German cookbook, Essen Wie Gott in Deutschland, *given to me by my daughter's former AFS host family, Rolf and Renata Brunswicker of Iserlohn, Germany. Due to my pitifully poor translation skill, and the infusion of local ingredients, the recipe is quite different from the original, but what attracted me was the beautiful presentation.*

This soup always draws raves as a first course for a brunch and works equally well as a unique dessert. The flavors are especially intense when served at room temperature, or just lukewarm; however, it is very refreshing served chilled on a warm summer day.

2 pounds tart apples (Gravenstein, Granny Smith, McIntosh)
1 cup port wine
3 cups Riesling wine
¾ cup sugar
3 tablespoons tapioca
1 3-inch stick cinnamon
½ teaspoon whole cloves
2 tablespoons pear brandy
½ cup heavy (whipping) cream
¼ cup finely ground toasted hazelnuts
1 tablespoon honey
• Mint leaves for garnish

Peel one or two apples and make 18 small apple balls with mellon-baller. Heat port wine to simmering. Place apple balls and wine in a glass or plastic container deep enough for the wine to cover the balls. Refrigerate overnight.

Fresh Apple Soup with Hazelnut-Apple Balls

Peel, core and slice remaining apples and place in a three to four quart saucepan along with the apple left over from making the balls. Add the Riesling wine, sugar, tapioca, cinnamon, and cloves. Cover and simmer, stirring occasionally, about 30 minutes or until apples are soft.

Remove cinnamon and cloves and force apples and liquid through a fine sieve; discard solids. Cool to room temperature and whisk in brandy and cream. Place one cup of the soup in a small bowl and mix with ¼ cup of the port wine that has been used for soaking the apple balls.

Remove the apple balls from the wine, drain, and—with the tip of a potato peeler—scoop out an indentation about ¼ inch wide and ½ inch deep in the center of each ball. Mix hazelnuts and honey together. Fill the cavity with nut mixture.

To serve, ladle the soup into flat soup dishes. Add a swirl of the port wine mixture, several apple balls, and a sprig of mint to each dish.

EASE OF PREPARATION: 2

PREPARATION TIME: 35 MINUTES

COOKING TIME: 30 MINUTES

SOAKING TIME: 8 HOURS

YIELD: 6 SERVINGS

PHOTO: OPPOSITE PAGE

NOTE: The thickness of the soup will depend somewhat on the type of apples used. If the soup is too thick, add a little bit more Riesling wine or light cream.

NOTE: To make the swirl in the soup, place the port wine mixture in a squeeze bottle and make a large "S" pattern. Drag a knife through the center. For a heart, make a circle and draw a knife through it.

Black Bean Soup with Hazelnut-Cilantro Pesto

EASE OF
PREPARATION: 2

PREPARATION TIME:
30 MINUTES

COOKING TIME:
2 TO 3 HOURS

YIELD:
8 TO 10 SERVINGS

PHOTO: PAGE 8

NOTE: Vegetable Stock (page 36) can be substituted for Chicken Stock (page 37).

NOTE: If chipotle peppers are not available in your area, substitute a canned or fresh jalapeño. Remember, the seeds are very hot. If a tamer version better suits your palate, mild green chilies may be used in place of the chipotle or jalapeño.

This black bean soup stands alone just fine, but it really comes to life with the Cilantro Pesto and garnishes. Leftovers are even better the second day.

1 pound (3 cups) dried black beans
• Water
2 tablespoons olive oil
1 medium onion, chopped (1 cup)
3 cloves garlic, minced
1 medium potato, peeled and diced in
    ½ inch pieces (1 cup)
1 28-ounce can crushed tomatoes
3 cups Chicken Stock (page 37)
1 medium canned chipotle pepper
    (smoked jalapeño)
½ teaspoon ground cumin
1 teaspoon salt, or to taste
• Freshly ground black pepper to taste
½ cup chopped fresh cilantro

Pick over beans, discarding any foreign material or blemished beans. Place in two to three quart saucepan and cover with cold water to at least two inches above beans. Place lid on saucepan, bring to a boil and simmer for at least one hour. Drain and rinse with fresh water.

Heat olive oil in three to four quart saucepan. Sauté onion and garlic until softened, about three minutes. Add cooked beans, potato, tomatoes, Chicken Stock (page 37), and chipotle. Season with cumin, salt, and freshly ground pepper. Simmer uncovered until beans are softened, about one to two hours, adding more stock if mixture becomes too thick. During the last 30 minutes of cooking, add cilantro and adjust the seasonings, adding more salt and pepper if desired.

Pesto

3 cloves garlic, peeled
1 cup cilantro leaves
½ cup grated parmesan cheese
½ cup finely chopped, toasted hazelnuts
⅓ cup olive oil

Place garlic in a food processor bowl fitted with a metal blade and pulse several times until finely minced. Add remaining ingredients and pulse several times until just well mixed. Transfer to small bowl.

To serve, ladle soup into serving dishes and stir about two teaspoons of the pesto into each bowl. Garnish with a dollop of sour cream, fresh tomatoes and another teaspoon of the pesto.

Garnish

• Sour cream
• Dried tomatoes
• Chopped cilantro

No hazelnut cookbook would be complete without a butternut squash and hazelnut recipe, as these two flavors seem to meld so well. This one has a different twist to it, with a hint of fruitiness and a crunch of bacon.

4 slices thick-sliced bacon

½ cup chopped onion

1 cup chopped celery

1 medium potato, peeled and diced (1 cup)

2 tart apples, peeled, seeded, chopped
    (Gravenstein, Granny Smith, etc.)
    (2 cups)

2 cups cooked yellow winter squash
    (Butternut, Sweet Dumpling, etc.)

4 cups Chicken Stock (page 37)

1 cup orange juice

1 cup heavy (whipping) cream

1 teaspoon salt

¼ teaspoon pepper

¼ teaspoon curry powder

1 cup coarsely chopped hazelnuts

In an 11-inch skillet with at least three-inch sides, fry bacon until crisp. Drain on paper towels. Crumble and set aside.

Pour off all but two tablespoons of the bacon fat. Over medium high heat, sauté onion until softened, about three minutes. Add celery, potato and apple, and continue cooking for another three minutes, stirring often. Mix in squash and Chicken Stock (page 37). Simmer for about 30 minutes or until vegetables are softened.

Creamy Squash & Bacon Soup

In a food processor fitted with a metal blade, process mixture until smooth, about 30 seconds, pureeing it in two batches if necessary. Return mixture to pan, adding orange juice, cream, salt, pepper and curry. Heat to simmering, adjust seasonings and add hazelnuts and reserved bacon.

TO COOK SQUASH IN MICROWAVE, cut squash in half lengthwise. Cover cut side with plastic film and place cut side down on plate. Cook on high until about half done. Let rest for several minutes and continue cooking until softened. Cooking time will vary in different ovens, but the general rule to follow is approximately seven minutes per pound.

TO COOK SQUASH IN OVEN, cut squash in half lengthwise. Place cut side down in a shallow baking pan. Add ½ inch water and bake in a 350-degree oven until softened, about 45 to 60 minutes, depending upon size of the squash.

EASE OF
PREPARATION: 2

PREPARATION TIME:
20 MINUTES
(NOT INCLUDING
STOCK)

COOKING TIME:
35 MINUTES

YIELD:
6 TO 8 SERVINGS

Cauliflower Soup with Hazelnut Garnish

EASE OF
PREPARATION: 2

PREPARATION TIME:
30 MINUTES

COOKING TIME:
40 MINUTES

YIELD:
8 - 1½ CUP SERVINGS

NOTE: Vegetable
Stock may be
substituted for
Chicken Stock
(page 37).

NOTE: The
cruciferous
vegetables—
cabbage, cauliflower,
broccoli, brussels
sprouts—are often
given a bum rap for
their pungent
cooking odor.
Sometimes this is
because the
vegetable is over-
mature, but often it
is from over-
cooking.

NOTE: Stocks can be
refrigerated for
serveral days or
frozen for up to two
months.

The delicate flavor of this soup showcases the toasted flavor of the hazelnuts that are used as a garnish in both the bottom and top of the bowl.

2 tablespoons vegetable oil
1 cup coarsely chopped onion
1 cup coarsely chopped celery
12 ounces cauliflower florets
2 medium potatoes, peeled and diced in
    ½ inch pieces
6 cups Chicken Stock (page 37)
1 teaspoon minced fresh thyme
    (½ teaspoon dried)
• Salt to taste
• Freshly ground black pepper to taste
1 cup tiny cauliflower florets
    (about ½ inch)
3 tablespoons butter
¼ cup all purpose flour
1 cup milk
1½ cups grated, medium cheddar cheese
    (about 6 ounces)
1 cup coarsely chopped toasted hazelnuts

In a four-quart saucepan, heat oil over medium high heat. Sauté onion and celery for about four minutes.

Break or cut cauliflower into one-inch pieces. Add to the pot along with potatoes, Chicken Stock (page 37), and thyme. Simmer uncovered for about 25 minutes or until cauliflower and potatoes are softened. Season with salt and pepper to taste.

With a potato masher, mash the soup so that most of the vegetables are crushed, forming a natural thickening. Add the tiny cauliflower florets and continue cooking for another ten minutes.

In the meantime, melt butter in small saucepan. Add flour and stir for several minutes, or until the mixture is a light golden color. Whisk in milk and cook over medium heat until the sauce is thickened, about two minutes. Remove from heat and whisk in cheddar cheese.

Pour sauce into the soup, stirring constantly. Continue cooking soup over medium heat until slightly thickened, about five minutes. Adjust seasonings.

To serve, place about one tablespoon of chopped hazelnuts in the bottom of each bowl. Add soup and sprinkle with an additional tablespoon of hazelnuts.

Vegetable Stock

1 tablespoon vegetable oil
1 clove garlic, minced
1 medium onion, coarsely chopped
2 medium carrots, coarsely chopped
2 ribs celery, coarsely chopped
3 medium fresh or canned tomatoes,
    chopped
½ cup dried mushrooms
    (Chanterelles, Shiitake, etc.)
¼ cup chopped parsley
¼ cup lentils
• Bouquet Garni
    (See page 31)
2 teaspoons salt
2½ quarts water

Heat oil in three or four quart kettle. Saute garlic, onion, carrots and celery for about five minutes, stirring often so the vegetables do not stick. Add the remaining ingredients, bring to a boil, reduce heat to low, and simmer—uncovered—for about one hour, or until liquid is reduced by about one quart. Strain liquid through a sieve and discard solids.

Taste the broth; if it tastes "watery" or does not have a good, intense flavor, return the liquid to the pot and continue cooking, uncovered, until the flavor intensifies to the desired taste. Stock is now ready for use.

Chicken & Dumplings Soup

If you like chicken and dumplings, you will love this soup. No bones, no fuss, and—as a bonus—low in fat. Use the bits and pieces of chicken left over from making stock.

Soup
1 tablespoon butter
½ cup coarsely chopped onion
1 cup coarsely chopped celery
1 cup bite-sized, cooked chicken pieces
6 cups Chicken Stock
1 cup fresh or frozen small green peas

In three or four quart kettle, heat butter until it starts to foam. Add onion and celery and sauté for about four minutes. Add chicken pieces and Chicken Stock (page 37). Bring to a boil and reduce heat to low. Simmer uncovered,for about ten minutes, or until celery is tender. Add peas and bring the liquid to a gentle simmer.

While the soup is simmering, make dumplings.

Dumplings
1 cup all purpose flour
1¼ teaspoons baking powder
½ teaspoon salt
½ cup coarsely chopped toasted hazelnuts
1 large egg
¼ cup milk

In a small bowl, whisk together flour, baking powder, and salt. Mix in hazelnuts. Whisk egg and milk together and stir into dry ingredients just until evenly moistened.

Dip a teaspoon into the simmering liquid. Scoop up a generous teaspoon of the dumpling batter and drop on top of the liquid. Repeat with remaining batter.

Cook covered for about four minutes; uncovered, for another four minutes. Serve immediately. However, leftovers will keep in the refrigerator overnight.

Chicken Stock
2 to 3 pounds raw chicken parts, cut up
    (necks, backs, wings, whole chicken)
1 medium onion, chopped
1 medium carrot, chopped
2 ribs celery, chopped (including tops)
• Bouquet Garni (see page 31)
2 teaspoons salt
• Water

Combine all ingredients in four to six quart soup or stock pot. Add cold water to cover by one inch. Over high heat, bring to boil, reduce heat, and simmer, uncovered, for about 1½ hours. During the first hour of cooking skim the scum off the top about every 15 minutes.

Strain through a sieve, and again through several layers of dampened cheesecloth. Discard vegetables and herbs. Pick meat off bones for use in other recipes.

Taste the broth; if it tastes "watery" or does not have a good, intense chicken flavor, return the liquid to the pot and continue cooking, uncovered, until the desired flavor develops.

Rapidly chill stock by placing the pot in a sink full of cold water, changing the water often until stock cools. Refrigerate until fat solidifies on top. Skim and discard fat. Stock is now ready for use.

NOTE: When there just isn't time to make homemade stock, commercial products may be used in these recipes. Mixing homemade and commercial stock, half and half, also gives soup a fresh flavor and helps stretch the budget.

EASE OF PREPARATION: 2

PREPARATION TIME: 20 MINUTES (NOT INCLUDING STOCK)

COOKING TIME: 20 MINUTES

YIELD: 6 TO 8 TWO-CUP SERVINGS

NOTE: Between each spoonful, dip teaspoon in the hot liquid so that the batter will slide off easily. In order to cook evenly, do not allow the dumplings to touch each other. Keep the liquid at a gentle simmer. The liquid should be moving, but the dumplings will toughen if cooked in rapidly boiling liquid.

NOTE: Stocks can be refrigerated for serveral days or frozen for up to two months.

Golden Onion Soup with Hazelnut Gratin

EASE OF
PREPARATION: 2

PREPARATION TIME:
20 MINUTES

COOKING TIME:
60 MINUTES

YIELD:
6 TO 8 SERVINGS

DID YOU KNOW...
That the hazelnut
was connected
with European
mythology and
witchcraft, and
even today many
people use a hazel
wand to locate
underground water.

This recipe is a refreshing change from the usual red wine/beef stock-based onion soups. The white wine and Chicken Stock (page 37) lighten and contrast nicely with the onions, and the nutty taste of a good Swiss cheese enhances the toasty flavor of the hazelnuts.

3 medium mild onions (4 cups sliced)
1 tablespoon olive oil
1 tablespoon butter
2 teaspoons granulated sugar
5 cups Chicken Stock (page 37)
1 cup dry white wine
    (Chardonnay, Chablis, etc.)
¼ teaspoon fresh ground black pepper
¼ cup all purpose flour
¼ cup cold water
• Salt to taste
• Grated Swiss cheese
    (Ementhaler, Jarlsberg)
½ cup coarsely chopped, toasted hazelnuts
¼ cup toasted bread crumbs

Peel onions and cut horizontally into ⅛-inch thick slices. Heat oil and butter in 11-inch skillet with three-inch sides (or any size pan that is large enough so that the onions are not crowded).

Add onions and, stirring frequently, sauté over medium heat until onions are a deep golden color, about ten minutes. During the last few minutes of cooking, sprinkle with sugar to help caramelize the onions, taking care not to burn.

Add Chicken Stock (page 37), white wine and pepper. Simmer for about 30 to 45 minutes, stirring occasionally. Whisk flour and water together to form a smooth paste. Rapidly stir mixture into the liquid. Simmer for another five minutes, stirring often. Taste and adjust seasonings, adding salt if necessary.

To serve, heat broiler. Ladle soup into broiler-safe bowls and top each serving with a generous sprinkling of Swiss cheese, hazelnuts and bread crumbs. Place bowls on a baking sheet and broil about three inches from the heat source for a minute or so, just until the cheese melts and the topping is browned. Serve immediately.

NOTE: In order for the onions to brown, be sure to use a pan that is wide enough that the onions are not crowded. If necessary, prepare in two batches and transfer to a four-quart kettle.

I cringe when I hear people say that they don't like fish because they can't stand that "fishy" smell. I do understand their concern, though. A fish that smells "fishy" will taste "fishy" and is past its prime.

A fresh ocean fish will have very little odor of its own. It will smell sweet and somewhat like fresh saltwater. Fish should be odor free, have firm flesh, and if whole, should have a clear, not cloudy eye.

Fish packaged in plastic wrap will develop a strong odor in a very short time. If prewrapped fish is purchased, remove from package, rinse with cold water, wrap in damp paper towels, and refrigerate.

Fish does not have the complicated muscle structure of red meat and should be cooked for a much shorter period of time. The most fool-proof method of cooking fish is to use the "Canadian Rule," named for the Canadian Department of Fisheries research. The Rule says to measure the fish at its thickest point, and cook 10 minutes per inch at recommended temperatures. This means that a fillet measuring 1" thick will take ten minutes to cook. This rule does not apply to shellfish, however, which generally take much less time to cook.

The fish should be close to room temperature—cooler fish will take longer. Double the time for frozen fish. To measure, lay the fish flat and measure at the thickest point.

Cook according to the following:

Bake	450 Degrees
Broil	Preheat Broiler
Pan fry	Medium high heat
Poach	Have liquid simmering
Barbecue	Have coals red hot; place fish several inches from coals.

The ten-minute-per-inch rule is quite accurate, but not fool proof. Sometimes a very dense fish will take a little longer. The fish is done when the flesh turns from translucent to opaque and it is slightly springy to the touch. Tuck the tail under if it is much thinner than the rest of the fish.

This very elegant presentation is perfect for that special occasion. Although there are several steps involved in the preparation, the mousse can be made in advance and refrigerated until baking time.

6 tablespoons toasted bread crumbs
6 tablespoons finely chopped
    toasted hazelnuts
3 tablespoons grated parmesan cheese
2 teaspoons vegetable oil
2 tablespoons chopped onion
2 ounces fresh spinach, washed,
    patted dry, and coarsely chopped
12 ounces fresh sea scallops
¾ cup heavy cream
1½ tablespoons fresh lemon juice
½ teaspoon salt
¼ teaspoon white pepper
6 ounces fresh salmon, bone and skin
    removed, cut into 1 inch chunks
1 teaspoon chopped fresh dill weed
4 egg whites, room temperature
½ teaspoon cream of tartar
• Butter to grease baking cups

In a small bowl mix together bread crumbs, hazelnuts, and parmesan cheese. Set aside.

In a small skillet, heat oil over medium high heat. Sauté onion until softened, about three minutes. Add spinach and stir until wilted, about two minutes. Cool.

In a food processor fitted with a metal blade, chop scallops. Add ½ cup cream and one tablespoon lemon juice. Process until mixture is smooth, adding ¼ teaspoon salt and ⅛ teaspoon white pepper. Transfer to one-quart mixing bowl.

Place salmon in same work bowl and process until finely chopped. Add the remaining cream, lemon juice, salt and pepper. Process until smooth. Transfer to another one-quart mixing bowl and fold in dill weed.

Wipe out work bowl and puree cooked onion and spinach.

Salmon, Scallop, & Spinach Mousse

Position a rack in the center of the oven and heat oven to 350 degrees.

Beat egg whites and cream of tartar until stiff peaks form. Fold about ⅔ of the egg whites into the scallop mixture and the remaining ⅓ into the salmon mixture. Place ⅓ of the scallop mixture in a small bowl and fold in chopped spinach.

Generously butter six ½-cup souffle or glass baking dishes. Dividing the mixture among the six dishes, first layer with the salmon mixture, then spinach, then scallop mixture. After each addition, smooth with the back of a spoon and gently tap on the counter to eliminate any air bubbles. Top with a sprinkling of parmesan/nut mixture.

Place cups about one inch apart on large baking sheet. Bake on center rack of a 350-degree oven for about 20 to 25 minutes or until centers are firm and tops spring back when lightly touched with fingertips.

Remove from oven and let stand several minutes. Run a knife around the edge of the cup to loosen mousse and unmold on the serving plate, salmon side up. Garnish with fresh dill weed and serve with a little Hazelnut Butter Sauce on the side.

Hazelnut Butter Sauce
¼ cup cold unsalted butter, divided
¼ cup finely chopped toasted hazelnuts
¼ cup dry, white wine
    (Chardonnay, Chablis, etc.)
1 teaspoon chopped fresh dill weed
    (¼ teaspoon dried)

Heat one tablespoon butter in saucepan. Add hazelnuts and toss until golden brown. Add wine and reduce by half. Remove from heat and stir in the remaining butter and dill.

EASE OF
PREPARATION: 3

PREPARATION TIME:
30 MINUTES.

COOKING TIME:
20 TO 25 MINUTES

YIELD:
8 ½-CUP SERVINGS

PHOTO:
OPPOSITE PAGE

Sautéed Halibut with Hazelnut-Lemon Sauce

EASE OF
PREPARATION: 1

PREPARATION TIME:
5 MINUTES

COOKING TIME:
8 MINUTES

YIELD: 4 SERVINGS

NOTE: If the more
flavorful flat-leafed
Italian parsley is
unavailable, the
curly-leafed variety
may be substituted.

David Machado, Executive Chef at Pazzo Ristorante, in Portland, Oregon, is one of the Northwest's premier chefs. Listed in Esquire *magazine as one of the "Chefs to Watch in 1995," he has also appeared on the national television program, "Great Chefs, Great Cities." He loves to share his knowledge of cooking by teaching classes when he has the opportunity.*

A champion of fresh regional ingredients, his pairing of halibut and hazelnuts in this recipe, which he generously shares, is a natural.

4 fresh halibut fillets, 6 ounces each
¼ cup all purpose flour
2 tablespoons olive oil
• Salt to taste
• Pepper to taste

Heat oven to 450 degrees.

Dredge the halibut fillet in flour; shake off excess. In a 10 to 12 inch oven-proof sauté pan, heat olive oil.

Season fish with salt and pepper and place in hot pan. Sauté on high heat for about two minutes per side, or until the fish is lightly browned on both sides.

Place pan in 450-degree oven for about six minutes or until the fish is firm to the touch. (See Intro to Fish, page 39). Remove from the oven and place on a warm platter.

Hazelnut-Lemon Sauce

¼ cup dry, white wine
   (Chablis, Chardonnay, etc.)
1 teaspoon finely chopped shallots
   (See Glossary, page 123-124)
6 ounces toasted, chopped hazelnuts
1 teaspoon fresh lemon juice
4 tablespoons cold unsalted butter
1 tablespoon chopped Italian parsley
½ teaspoon lemon zest
   (See Glossary, pages 123-124)

To make the sauce, over high heat, deglaze the pan with white wine. Add shallots, hazelnuts, and lemon juice and reduce until the liquid is slightly syrupy. Remove pan from the heat and whisk in the cold butter, parsley, and lemon zest. Stir until sauce is thickened.

PRESENTATION TIP: Serve the halibut on a bed of sautéed spinach and pour the sauce over the fish. Garnish with long strands of lemon zest.

Even if you don't like oysters, try them this way . . . you may change your mind.

2 whole eggs, slightly beaten
½ teaspoon hot pepper sauce
1 pint small or extra small fresh oysters, drained
1 cup all purpose white flour
1½ cups chopped hazelnuts
1 cup finely chopped green onions
1 tablespoon olive oil
1 tablespoon butter
• Salt to taste
• Pepper to taste
• Fresh lemon wedges

Whisk hot pepper sauce into beaten eggs. Dip oysters first in egg and then coat with flour. Place on a dry platter and let stand for about ten minutes or until the egg and flour sit long enough to make a "glue." In another plate, mix hazelnuts and green onions together. Press oysters into the mixture, coating on both sides.

Heat oil and butter in large skillet. Sauté oysters over medium high heat just until golden, about one to two minutes on each side. Season with salt, pepper, and a squirt of fresh lemon juice. Add more oil and butter if necessary to fry remaining oysters. Serve with Tarter Sauce, if desired.

Pan Fried Oysters Encrusted with Toasted Hazelnuts

Tarter Sauce
¾ cup mayonnaise
¼ cup sour cream
⅓ cup finely chopped dill pickle
2 tablespoons finely chopped onion
1 tablespoon minced parsley
1 tablespoon capers
   (See Glossary, pages 123-124)
1 to 2 tablespoons fresh lemon juice
• Dash freshly ground black pepper

Combine all ingredients and refrigerate several hours for flavors to blend.

NOTE: The secret to getting the coating to stay on the oysters is in first making the "glue." This is accomplished by allowing the oysters to rest after coating in egg and flour. Try not to disturb them any more than necessary once they are in the pan. Brown well on one side, carefully flip over, and most of the coating will stay on.

Also, be sure to use enough oil to keep them from sticking—and don't crowd them in the pan.

EASE OF PREPARATION: 2

PREPARATION AND RESTING TIME: 18 MINUTES

COOKING TIME: 4 MINUTES PER BATCH

YIELD: 4 TO 6 SERVINGS

NOTE: Really fresh oysters should be sweet and buttery, with an aroma reminiscent of fresh ocean breezes. As oysters develop their own distinctive flavor from the waters in which they are grown, there will be subtle differences in flavor from bay to bay.

Northwest Crab Cakes

EASE OF
PREPARATION: 1

PREPARATION TIME:
10 MINUTES

COOKING TIME:
5 MINUTES

YIELD:
8 TO 10 PATTIES,
4 SERVINGS

In the Northwest, when reference is made to crab, it unquestionably refers to Dungeness Crab. No other crab can compare to the sweet, succulent flavor of this Pacific jewel. Although purists find it hard to eat fresh crab dressed with little more than a fresh lemon, this recipe will win some converts. There are no fancy ingredients, just fresh flavors, enhanced by the toasty hazelnuts.

1 pound Dungeness crab meat (2 cups)
2 cups cracker crumbs
½ cup mayonnaise
⅓ cup finely chopped green onions
⅓ cup chopped toasted hazelnuts
¼ cup finely diced green pepper
2 tablespoons fresh lemon juice
1 egg, slightly beaten
2 tablespoons chopped fresh parsley
• Freshly ground black pepper to taste
• Vegetable oil for frying

In a two-quart bowl, mix together all ingredients, up through the black pepper. Form into ½ inch thick patties.

In 10 to 12 inch frying pan, heat about one tablespoon oil over medium high heat. Fry patties, turning once, just until they are golden, about one minute per side. Do not crowd in pan. If necessary, add more oil and fry in two batches.

NOTE: Tip from my good friend, Rod Purdy, who owns Fitts Seafood Market in Salem, Oregon . . . When the price of Dungeness crab exceeds your budget, stretch it with cooked white fish such as ling cod or true cod. These two fish have textures that are the closest to crab meat.

Steam the fish in water and white vinegar, ⅓ cup vinegar to one cup water. (The vinegar helps sweeten the fish.) Remove from poaching liquid. Cool, remove any bones, flake, and combine equal amounts of fish and Dungeness crab meat and juice. Cover and refrigerate overnight. Use as fresh crab meat.

I find this works best with fresh, whole crab in the shell, rather than with pre-shelled crab meat, as the whole crab has more juices that flavor the white fish.

Roasted Red Pepper Sauce

2 whole red peppers
1 small jalapeño pepper
2 tablespoons Italian parsley
    (can substitute curly)
1 large clove garlic
1 tablespoon olive oil
1 tablespoon lime juice
• Pinch salt

Heat broiler to high.

Slice red peppers and jalapeño pepper in half horizontally. Remove seeds and membrane. Place cut side down on broiler pan and broil about three inches from the heat source until the peppers are black and soft. Blacking time will vary with the thickness and size of pepper, but approximately four to five minutes for jalapeño and six to eight minutes for red peppers. Immediately place in paper bag, close tightly, and let steam for about ten minutes. Remove blackened skins and discard. Chop pepper in small pieces.

While preparing peppers, mince parsley and garlic in food processor bowl fitted with metal blade. Add chopped peppers and remaining ingredients and puree.

The Yellow Fin or "Ahi", as it is often called, is the premier tuna for grilling and broiling. With its firm texture and dark pink color, it is often referred to as the beefsteak of the fish world. Most well-stocked fish markets carry Ahi, but if not, try this recipe with fresh Albacore tuna or even halibut.

¼ cup soy sauce
2 tablespoons brown sugar
2 cloves garlic, minced
2 teaspoons minced fresh ginger
1 tablespoon vegetable oil
4 Yellow Fin tuna steaks,
    about 4 to 5 ounces each, ¾ inch thick
1 tablespoon chopped green peppercorns
¼ cup coarsely chopped toasted hazelnuts

In a one-gallon plastic bag, combine soy sauce, brown sugar, garlic, ginger, and vegetable oil. Place tuna steaks in bag and refrigerate for at least two hours, or up to overnight. Remove from marinade; pat dry.

Yellow Fin Tuna with Green Peppercorns & Hazelnuts

Heat grill or barbecue until very hot. Grill tuna for several minutes on each side, just until it is browned on the outside, but still pink in the center. The timing will depend upon the heat of the grill, but generally the Canadian Rule is a good one—ten minutes per inch of fish. (See Intro to Fish, page 39).

Serve the fish with a sprinkling of green peppercorns and chopped hazelnuts.

NOTE: Green peppercorns are found in the condiment section of most grocery stores.

EASE OF
PREPARATION: 1

PREPARATION TIME:
5 MINUTE

MARINATING TIME:
2 HOURS, PLUS

COOKING TIME:
8 MINUTES

YIELD: 4 SERVINGS

This recipe is a lighter way to do fish for fish and chips. It is a good way to use up small, uneven pieces.

1 pound boned whitefish,
    about 1 inch thick (halibut or cod)
2 tablespoons fresh lemon juice
1 teaspoon fresh dill weed
    (½ teaspoon dried)
½ cup all purpose white flour
½ cup finely chopped toasted hazelnuts
1 egg white, slightly beaten
• Vegetable oil for frying
• Salt to taste
• Freshly ground black pepper to taste

Rinse fish with cold water; pat dry with paper towels. Cut into one-inch-square chunks; rub with lemon juice and dill weed.

Hazelnut Batter Fried Fish

In a small bowl mix flour and hazelnuts together.

Dip fish into egg white and then into flour and hazelnut mixture. Place on clean plate and let stand for about five minutes.

Heat several tablespoons of oil in a skillet over medium high heat. When the oil is hot, drop fish chunks into the skillet. Fry until golden, about one to two minutes on all four sides, reducing heat if the crust becomes too brown. Season with salt and pepper. The fish is done when it is firm to the touch and is no longer translucent.

Serve with Tarter Sauce, page 43.

EASE OF
PREPARATION: 1

PREPARATION TIME:
10 MINUTES

COOKING TIME:
8 TO 10 MINUTES

YIELD:
4 SERVINGS

Seared Salmon Fillets with Fennel Sauce

The slight hint of sweetness from the apple and fennel compliment the buttery flavor of the salmon. Excellent served with Risotto with Spinach, Hazelnuts and Mushrooms, page 60.

5 tablespoons cold unsalted butter, divided
4 4-ounce boneless, skinless
     fresh salmon fillets
• Salt to taste
• Pepper to taste
1 tablespoon chopped shallots
     (See Glossary, pages 123-124)
1 cup coarsely diced fresh fennel
     (1 medium bulb)
½ cup Chicken Stock (page 37)
     or fish stock
1 tablespoon apple juice concentrate
1 teaspoon chopped fresh tarragon
     (½ teaspoon dried)
¼ cup medium chopped toasted hazelnuts

Heat oven to 450 degrees.

Melt one tablespoon of the butter in a 10 to 12 inch skillet. Over medium high heat, sear salmon on both sides, about one to two minutes per side. Season with salt and pepper.

Place on an oven-proof serving platter or pan and bake in a 450-degree oven for about eight to ten minutes, depending upon the thickness of the fish (see Introduction to Fish, page 39) or until the fish is just barely firm when pressed at the thickest part.

In the meantime, place shallots and fennel in the skillet. Over medium heat toss until well coated with the pan drippings. Add fish stock or Chicken Stock (page 37) and apple juice concentrate. Cook, stirring often, until the fennel is tender and the liquid is almost evaporated. Add a little more stock if necessary. Remove the pan from the heat and whisk in remaining cold butter, one tablespoon at a time, until a sauce is formed. Whisk in tarragon.

To serve, pour sauce over fish and sprinkle with hazelnuts. Garnish with additional tarragon or fennel leaves.

Probably the most challenging part of cooking meat and poultry is in determining when it is done. Overcooking sometimes produces an unpleasant tough, leathery texture. Undercooking sometimes can present a real health hazard.

An instant-read thermometer, which can be purchased at almost any kitchen store, is an indispensable tool in the kitchen. Just insert into the thickest part of the meat, being careful not to touch a bone, and in a few seconds get the reading. To make sure the thermometer is accurate, plunge it in boiling water. If it does not register exactly 212 degrees Fahrenheit (at sea level), make an adjustment by adding or subtracting a few degrees if necessary.

It is not quite as easy when the meat is too thin to insert the thermometer. In this case, sight and touch are the best tools. When touched in the center the meat should spring back. If it is soft it very likely needs more cooking. If not sure, cut a piece open with a knife to check for doneness.

For safety's sake, wash any surface, including your hands, that comes in contact with the meat or poultry with hot, soapy water.

This recipe, which appears on the cover, is quick, fresh and easy. Serve with Hazelnut Pilaf and Salad of Fresh Pear, Greens, & Honeyed Hazelnuts, which are also on the cover.

Turkey Breast with Colored Peppers & Hazelnut Dijon Sauce

1 pound turkey tenderloin,
   or 2-inch round portion of breast meat
• Flour for dredging
• Salt to taste
• Freshly ground black pepper to taste
1 tablespoon butter
1 tablespoon vegetable oil
¼ red onion, cut in ¼-inch strips
½ each red, yellow and green pepper,
   cut in ¼-inch strips (about 1½ cups)
2 cups Chicken Stock (page 37)
⅓ cup dry, white wine
   (Chardonnay, Chablis, etc.)
½ cup heavy (whipping) cream
2 teaspoons dijon-style mustard
1 teaspoon chopped fresh thyme
   (½ teaspoon dried)
⅓ cup coarsely chopped toasted hazelnuts

Prepare the turkey by slicing in ½-inch-thick rounds (about one ounce each). Place between two sheets of plastic wrap and flatten by pressing with the palm of the hand to about ¼ inch thick. Dredge with flour, shake off excess, and season with salt and pepper.

In a 10 to 12 inch skillet, heat butter and oil over medium high heat. Sauté turkey pieces on both sides until they are golden and the meat turns an opaque white color, about one minute per side. Do not over-cook or the meat will be tough. Remove to a plate, and keep warm.

Add onion and colored peppers to the same skillet and toss for about two to three minutes, adding more oil if necessary, just until partially cooked. Remove to a plate, and keep warm.

Increase heat to high and add Chicken Stock (page 37) and wine to skillet. Cook until liquid is reduced by about half. Add cream and, again, reduce by half. Total reduction time should be about five minutes. Whisk in mustard and thyme and continue cooking for several minutes. Stir in hazelnuts.

TO SERVE: Place about three to four turkey slices on a place, spoon onion and peppers on the side and drizzle with several tablespoons of the sauce.

EASE OF
PREPARATION: 2

PREPARATION TIME:
10 MINUTES

COOKING TIME:
10 MINUTES

YIELD:
SERVES 4 TO 6

PHOTO:
SEE FRONT COVER

Medallions of Pork, Shanghai

EASE OF
PREPARATION: 2

PREPARATION TIME:
20 MINUTES

COOKING TIME:
10 MINUTES

YIELD: SERVES 4

PHOTO: PAGE 48

The crunch of hazelnuts adds an interesting dimension to this refreshing sweet/sour, citrus dish. Cook the rice while preparing the main portion of the recipe.

2 tablespoons frozen
    orange juice concentrate
2 tablespoons soy sauce
1 tablespoon vinegar
2 tablespoons brown sugar
2 teaspoons grated fresh ginger
2 teaspoons cornstarch
½ teaspoon sesame oil
• Pinch crushed hot, red pepper flakes
⅓ cup water
1 pork tenderloin (8 ounces),
    sliced in ½-inch-thick pieces
2 teaspoons vegetable oil
• Salt to taste
• Pepper to taste
6 green onions, diagonally sliced
1 cup whole, fresh pea pods,
    stems removed
½ cup fresh red pepper strips
½ cup fresh green pepper strips
½ cup fresh or canned, drained
    mandarin orange slices
3 cups cooked long grain, white rice
½ cup coarsely chopped hazelnuts
¼ cup chopped parsley

In a small bowl, whisk together orange juice concentrate, soy sauce, vinegar, brown sugar, ginger, cornstarch, sesame oil, red peppers, and water. Set aside.

Trim fat from pork and slice into ½-inch rounds. Place meat between two sheets of plastic wrap and press with palm of hand until ¼ inch thick. Heat oil in wok or skillet. Over medium high heat, brown pork on both sides, and cook just until meat is firm and white, about three minutes. Season with salt and pepper and remove from skillet. Place green onions, pea pods, and peppers in skillet and stir just until heated through, about two minutes. Remove from skillet and add to meat.

Pour sauce into skillet and simmer until slightly thickened. Return meat and vegetables to skillet, toss with the sauce. Add mandarin orange slices, and spoon mixture over cooked rice. Sprinkle with hazelnuts and parsley.

White Rice
2 cups cold water
1 teaspoon salt
1 teaspoon vegetable oil
1 cup long grain white rice

In a two-quart saucepan, bring water, salt, and oil to a boil. Add rice, and return to a boil. Reduce heat to simmer. Cook uncovered until most of the liquid evaporates and steam holes, or "rice eyes" appear, about ten minutes. Cover and continue to simmer for several minutes until rice is tender and liquid disappears. Let stand, covered, for several minutes. Fluff with fork and serve.

NOTE: Do not stir rice during the cooking process or it will become sticky. Cooking times will vary with the age and variety of the rice. Makes three cups of cooked rice.

If you prefer not to eat the skin of the chicken, remove it after cooking. Retaining the skin during the cooking process helps keep the moisture in the meat and adds very little fat. Fresh asparagus makes a nice accompaniment to this recipe. The stuffing may also be used to stuff a boneless turkey breast.

1 tablespoon butter or vegetable oil

¼ cup finely chopped onion

1½ cups finely chopped mushrooms

¾ cup finely chopped celery

1½ cups soft bread crumbs

1 cup cooked Wild Rice
   (See page 61)

½ cup dried cranberries

½ cup coarsely chopped toasted hazelnuts

1 teaspoon minced fresh thyme
   (½ teaspoon dried)

½ teaspoon minced fresh sage
   (¼ teaspoon dried)

½ teaspoon salt

⅛ teaspoon freshly ground black pepper

4 chicken breast halves, boned

2 teaspoons vegetable oil

Heat butter or oil in a 10 to 12 inch skillet. Over medium high heat, sauté onion until softened, about three minutes. Add mushrooms and continue cooking, stirring often, until most of the moisture has evaporated, about five minutes. Transfer to a large mixing bowl and add remaining ingredients up through the pepper. Mix well to distribute the ingredients evenly.

Chicken Breasts with Cranberry & Hazelnut Stuffing

Wash the skillet to sauté the chicken breasts.

With a sharp knife, cut a two-inch slit horizontally, about one inch deep, in the center of the chicken breast. With the knife, or index finger in the slit, pull it further open to make a pocket that extends to within ½ inch of the edges of the meat. Fill the pocket loosely with several tablespoons stuffing. Heat oven to 350 degrees.

Heat the vegetable oil in the skillet, over medium high heat. Place the stuffed breasts, skin side down in the hot skillet and sauté just until brown, about three to four minutes per side. Transfer the browned chicken to a shallow baking pan, and spoon the remaining stuffing beside the poultry. Cover the stuffing loosely with foil so the wild rice does not dry out. Remove the foil during the last five minutes of baking. Bake in a 350-degree oven for about 20 minutes, or until the meat reaches 165 degrees and the tops are nicely browned.

PRESENTATION TIP: Serve the extra stuffing in hollowed-out orange cups. It looks pretty and adds a hint of orange flavoring.

EASE OF
PREPARATION: 3

PREPARATION TIME:
25 MINUTES

COOKING TIME:
20 MINUTES

YIELD: 4 SERVINGS

NOTE: Dried cranberries can be obtained in most well stocked grocery, specialty and bulk food stores.

NOTE: Both the chicken and the stuffing may be prepared in advance; however, do not stuff the chicken until shortly before cooking.

Stove Top Layered Casserole

EASE OF
PREPARATION: 1

PREPARATION TIME:
20 MINUTES

COOKING TIME:
30 MINUTES

SPECIAL
EQUIPMENT:
DUTCH OVEN OR
HEAVY SKILLET
WITH 4-INCH-HIGH
SIDES AND LID

YIELD: 6 SERVINGS

One of Portland's most innovative cooks, Betty Shenberger's creative recipes have won numerous awards in cooking contests. In this recipe, she combines everyday ingredients into a striking and unusual dish.

Betty likes to cook and serve this casserole in a pretty enamel dutch oven.

1 tablespoon butter
6 medium California White or
    Yukon Gold potatoes, scrubbed
    and sliced in ¼ inch thick slices
1½ cups seasoned Chicken Stock (page 37)
½ head green cabbage, thinly sliced
    (about 4 to 5 cups)
1 cup sliced green onions
• Salt to taste
• Pepper to taste
3 ¼-inch thick slices boneless ham
2 ¼-inch thick slices Swiss cheese
6 to 8 very thin slices hard, dry salami
1 cup coarsely chopped toasted hazelnuts

Over medium high heat, melt butter in a four-quart nonstick dutch oven or heavy skillet with high sides and a tight lid. Add potatoes and toss to coat with butter. Level out the potatoes and add Chicken Stock (page 37). Cover and cook until the stock is bubbling, reduce heat, and simmer for about 15 minutes. Potatoes should be slightly underdone.

Layer with cabbage and green onions. Season with salt and pepper. Cover and continue cooking for about ten minutes, or until vegetables are tender.

Meanwhile, julienne the ham, Swiss, and salami in quarter-inch matchsticks. Finish layering with ham, Swiss cheese, and salami. Cover for about five minutes to melt the cheese. Sprinkle with hazelnuts. Serve in the cooking pan.

NOTE: If desired, drizzle a little Vinaigrette. Caraway seeds are also a nice optional addition.

Vinaigrette
1 clove garlic, minced
¼ cup olive oil
¼ cup vegetable oil
3 to 4 tablespoons balsamic vinegar
1 tablespoon minced fresh tarragon
    (1 teaspoon dried)
1 teaspoon dijon mustard
1 teaspoon honey
• Pinch salt
• Pinch red pepper flakes
• Freshly ground black pepper to taste

With a whisk or a mini-chop, mix all ingredients together until creamy.

NOTE: Keep Vinaigrette in the refrigerator for tossed salads and as a nice addition to the Stove Top Casserole (See page 52).

The creamy tomatillo sauce is a nice change from traditional red sauce. This can also be made as a layered casserole with repeating layers of tortillas, chicken, sauce, cheese, and nuts.

1 lb. fresh or 1 12-ounce can tomatillos
2 cloves garlic, peeled
2 jalapeño peppers, seeded
    (about 2 teaspoons....or more!)
2 tablespoons cilantro leaves
2 tablespoons onion
⅔ cup sour cream
1 tablespoon honey
¼ teaspoon salt
⅓ cup canned diced green chilies, drained
8 corn tortillas
1½ cups cooked shredded chicken
2 to 3 cups shredded jack cheese
    (about 6 ounces)
1 cup coarsely chopped toasted hazelnuts

If using fresh tomatillos, prepare by washing and removing husks. Place in saucepan, cover with water, and simmer until tender, about five to seven minutes; drain. If using canned tomatillos, drain and discard the liquid.

Spicy Chicken & Hazelnut Enchiladas

Sauce

Mince garlic, jalapeños, cilantro, and onion in a food processor or blender. Add drained tomatillos, sour cream, honey, and salt; puree. Mix in green chilies and set aside.

Tortillas

Soften tortillas either by wrapping in foil and placing in hot oven until warm, or by covering loosely with plastic wrap and placing in microwave oven until heated.

Divide chicken among the tortillas, add about two tablespoons each of sauce and cheese. Sprinkle each with about two teaspoons chopped hazelnuts, and roll tortilla around the filling.

Pour ¼ of the remaining sauce in the bottom of a greased 9 x 12 baking dish. Place filled enchiladas in the dish, seam side down, and pour remaining sauce over top. Sprinkle with remaining cheese and then with hazelnuts.

Bake in 350 oven until heated through, about 20 minutes.

EASE OF
PREPARATION: 2

PREPARATION TIME:
25 MINUTES.

BAKING TIME:
20 MINUTES.

YIELD:
8 ENCHILADAS

LOW FAT TIP:
Replace all or half the sour cream with plain yogurt. (A reduced fat cheese may also be used.) If using yogurt, however, be careful not to over-heat the sauce or it will break down. To reduce the liquid in yogurt, place the yogurt in a strainer lined with a coffee filter. Hook the strainer over a bowl and refrigerate overnight. Some liquid will drip into the bowl, giving the yogurt a firmer, more cheese-like texture. Commercial "Yogurt Cheese" filters are also available in kitchen stores.

Teriyaki Beef Stir Fry

EASE OF
PREPARATION: 1

PREPARATION TIME:
10 MINUTES

MARINATING TIME:
2 HOURS PLUS

COOKING TIME:
8 TO 10 MINUTES

YIELD:
4 TO 6 SERVINGS.

NOTE: For an interesting variation, add cream sherry instead of water to the cornstarch thickening.

Stir fry is to today's cooking what casseroles were to the 50s. It is quick to fix and limited only by the cook's imagination. Very little meat is needed and a few extra vegetables can always stretch to cover one more diner.

8 ounces sirloin steak
1/3 cup teriyaki sauce
2 teaspoons grated fresh ginger
• Pinch dried hot red pepper flakes
2 tablespoons vegetable oil
2 cloves garlic, minced
2 medium carrots,
   peeled and sliced into thin rounds
1 cup broccoli florets
1 cup sliced mushrooms (2½ ounces)
4 green onions, sliced in 1 inch pieces
½ of a red pepper, sliced in long thin slices
½ of a green pepper,
   sliced in long thin slices
2 teaspoons cornstarch
• Freshly ground black pepper to taste
½ cup coarsely chopped toasted hazelnuts

Slice beef into thin strips, about 1½ inches long and ¼-inch thick. In a plastic bag, combine teriyaki sauce, ginger, red pepper flakes and one tablespoon of the oil. Add meat and refrigerate for at least one hour, or up to eight hours. Drain and reserve marinade.

Heat remaining oil in wok or large skillet. Over medium high heat sauté meat and garlic together. Remove meat when browned and keep warm. Stir fry vegetables, one at a time in the order given, until tender crisp, adding more oil if necessary. Return meat to pan. Stir cornstarch into reserved marinade, adding water to make 1/3 cup. Add mixture to pan and toss with vegetables, stirring until slightly thickened and heated through. Season with freshly ground black pepper. Sprinkle with hazelnuts and serve over rice if desired.

NOTE: To cook White Rice, see page 50. To cook Brown Rice, see page 61.

TIME SAVER: Partially cook carrots and broccoli in microwave, then stir fry for added flavor.

This is a nice company recipe. It is good served with the Sweet Potato and Cranberry Gratin on page 71.

1 cup dried bread crumbs
    (See Glossary, pages 123-124)
½ cup coarsely chopped, toasted hazelnuts
½ cup freshly grated parmesan cheese
2 tablespoons softened butter
1 tablespoon dijon mustard
2 cloves garlic, minced
2 teaspoons chopped, fresh rosemary
    (1 teaspoon dried leaves)
1 teaspoon dried ground sage
½ teaspoon salt
⅛ teaspoon freshly ground black pepper
1 to 1½ pound piece boneless pork loin,
    about 3 inches thick

Preheat oven to 425 degrees.

In medium bowl, mix together all ingredients except pork loin. Set aside.

Remove any visible fat from pork. Butterfly by slitting lengthwise down the center of the loin, cutting to within ½ inch of the bottom. From the center cut, slice sides in half, horizontally, to within ½ inch of the edges; lay flat.

Loin of Pork with Hazelnuts, Parmesan, & Rosemary

Spread ½ of the mixture on flattened meat. Fold sides over filling and place, cut side down, on ungreased shallow baking sheet. Pat the remaining mixture evenly over the tops and sides of the meat. Bake on the center rack of a preheated, 425-degree oven for 20 minutes.

Reduce heat to 350 degrees and continue cooking until crust is golden and the internal temperature reaches 160 degrees, about 20 minutes.

Remove from the oven and let rest ten minutes before slicing.

EASE OF
PREPARATION: 3

PREPARATION TIME:
20 MINUTES

BAKING AND
RESTING TIME:
50 MINUTES

YIELD:
6 TO 8 SERVINGS

NOTE: Resting time is important for baked meats. It gives the juices time to settle, firms up the meat and makes slicing much easier.

NOTE: If more stuffing is desired, the recipe can be doubled. It also makes a good filling for stuffed mushrooms.

Turkey Nut Burgers

EASE OF
PREPARATION: 1

PREPARATION TIME:
10 MINUTES

COOKING TIME:
5 MINUTES

YIELD:
6 PATTIES

DID YOU KNOW . . .
That hazelnuts have
a richer, more
intense flavor and
sweetness than
other nuts.

These burgers are delicious in a good, chewy bun topped with whole cranberry sauce and any of the fixings of the "other" burger. Or you may want to try them, minus the bun, served with Lemon Mayonnaise.

1 pound ground turkey meat
½ cup fresh bread crumbs
⅓ cup coarsely chopped, toasted hazelnuts
¼ cup coarsely chopped fresh
    or frozen cranberries
¼ cup chopped celery
2 tablespoons minced onion
2 tablespoons minced fresh parsley
½ teaspoon dried ground sage
1 large egg, slightly beaten
1 teaspoon salt
• Several grinds freshly ground
    black pepper

Thoroughly mix all ingredients in a large bowl. Form into six patties and either broil about three inches from the heat for about two minutes on each side, or sauté in a small amount of vegetable oil about two minutes per side or until they are browned, firm, and an opaque white color at the center.

Lemon Mayonnaise
½ cup good quality mayonnaise
1 tablespoon lemon juice
1 tablespoon minced fresh parsley

In a small bowl whisk ingredients together. Refrigerate.

With most trendy foods, today's stars are tomorrow's has-beens. This is not true, however, with pasta, or noodles, if you prefer.

Even though quite a few home pasta machines are now gathering dust, pasta still remains one of our favorite foods. We just rarely seem to have time to make it from scratch.

Although the following pasta recipes call for dried pasta, by all means use fresh if it is available. There is no doubt that fresh is better, but then again, it isn't always there when you need it. Remember that fresh pasta cooks in a fraction of the time needed for dried pasta.

When cooking pasta, it is important to have plenty of boiling water. The noodles need plenty of room to move around in so that they cook evenly. Cook "al dente," until they are tender, but still slightly resistant to the bite.

To rinse or not is a topic for contention, but personally, I like to rinse with cold water when making cold pasta dishes. Tossing with a few drops of olive oil will probably do more, though, to prevent sticking. With hot dishes, however, it doesn't hurt to have a little extra "glue" to help the sauce stick. Adding oil to the cooking water does little good as it is just poured off and little clings to the pasta.

Toasted hazelnuts add a nice touch when teamed with pasta and grains. Added just before serving, the crunch of the nuts adds a nice contrast to the smoothness of the grain.

Grecian Pasta

Like Oregon, Greece is a producer of hazelnuts, so it seemed natural to add hazelnuts to a Greek inspired dish. This dish contains many assertive flavors, but they all blend well together.

2 tablespoons olive oil, divided
2 cloves garlic, minced
½ thinly sliced red pepper
½ thinly sliced yellow pepper
½ thinly sliced green pepper
2 large ripe tomatoes, peeled, seeded, and
    diced in ½ inch pieces (2 cups)
4 ounces soft goat cheese (Chévre)
• Cooked Penne pasta
½ cup coarsely chopped toasted hazelnuts
½ cup cooked artichoke hearts, quartered
½ cup Kalamata or Sicilian olives*
¼ cup chopped fresh basil
2 tablespoons fresh lemon juice
• Freshly ground black pepper to taste

In a large skillet, heat one tablespoon olive oil. Over medium heat, sauté garlic until softened, about two minutes. Add peppers and sauté for another two minutes. Add tomatoes and stir just until they release their juices, about two minutes. Stir in goat cheese to make a creamy sauce.

Toss with cooked pasta, hazelnuts, artichokes, olives, and basil. Drizzle with lemon juice and remaining olive oil. Season with freshly ground black pepper to taste.

* NOTE: If these two types of olives are unavailable, any other brine-cured olive may be substituted.

TIP: To peel tomatoes, spear the stem end with a fork. Holding the fork, immerse tomato in boiling water for about one minute. Cool by holding the tomato in a stream of cold water. The peel should slip off easily.

TIP: To seed tomatoes, cut in half horizontally. Place one half in the palm of your hand like you were holding a baseball for an overhand throw. Firmly squeeze at the same time, making a downward throwing motion over the sink or waste basket. Most of the seeds will come out. Just don't let loose!

Penne Pasta
2½ quarts water
2 teaspoons salt
8 to 10 ounces Penne pasta

In a four-quart kettle bring water to boil. Add salt and pasta, stir, and cook until just barely tender, about eight to ten minutes. Drain and rinse, if desired.

EASE OF
PREPARATION: 2

PREPARATION TIME:
15 MINUTES

COOKING TIME:
15 MINUTES

YIELD:
6 TO 8 SERVINGS

PHOTO:
OPPOSITE PAGE

NOTE: Cooked, fresh artichokes are delicious in this recipe; however, canned or marinated work well too. If using marinated, be sure to take a paper towel and pat off the marinade before using.

NOTE: For Goat Cheese (Chévre) see page 19.

Risotto with Spinach, Hazelnuts, & Mushrooms

NOTE: Arborio rice
is traditionally used
in making risotto.
It is found in most
Italian markets
or well-stocked
supermarkets and
specialty stores.
Regular, long-
grained rice may be
substituted, but the
texture will not be
quite as creamy.

NOTE: A 4½-ounce
can or jar of drained
button or specialty
mushrooms may be
used in place of the
fresh.

Risotto has a soft, creamy texture that is different from the way Americans are accustomed to eating rice, with each kernel separate. This consistency is due to the high starch content of the Arborio rice and because the liquid is added, small amounts at a time, and stirred often. Risotto takes a little attention, but you can go ahead and prepare the remaining ingredients while it is simmering—just keep an eye and a hand on the pot!

2¼ cups (approximate) Chicken Stock
    (page 37)
½ cup dry white wine
    (Chablis, Chardonnay, etc.)
3 tablespoons butter, divided
1 cup sliced mushrooms (2½ ounces)
1 small onion, chopped (½ cup)
1 cup Arborio rice
1 medium tomato, seeded and diced
    (See note on page 59 on how to seed)
2 ounces fresh spinach,
    sliced in ⅛-inch strips
• Salt to taste
• Freshly ground black pepper to taste
¼ cup chopped, toasted hazelnuts
⅓ cup grated parmesan cheese

In a two-quart saucepan or microwave oven, combine Chicken Stock (page 37) and wine. Heat to simmering. Heat one tablespoon of the butter in a large skillet. Over medium high heat sauté mushrooms until golden, about four to five minutes. Remove from the skillet and reserve.

Add another tablespoon of butter to skillet; sauté onion until softened, about three to four minutes. Add rice and stir for several minutes until the grains are well coated with butter and start to turn golden.

Turn heat to low and add ¼ cup warm stock; stir until rice has absorbed most of the liquid. Add the remaining stock ¼ cup at a time, stirring after each addition, until the rice has absorbed the liquid and is tender and creamy, approximately 30 minutes. (After each ¼-cup addition, it should be stirred until almost all liquid is absorbed). The rice should be creamy on the outside, and slightly firm in the center. Add additional stock, if necessary, to obtain this consistency.

Stir in reserved mushrooms, tomatoes, and spinach. Season with salt and pepper to taste. Stir in remaining one tablespoon butter, hazelnuts, and parmesan cheese.

Hazelnut, Mushroom, & Wild Rice Pilaf

The earthy flavor of toasted hazelnuts is a natural with both brown and wild rice. Adding cooked poultry, seafood, or vegetables will stretch this recipe into a main dish meal.

2 teaspoons butter
2 teaspoons vegetable oil
1 cup sliced mushrooms (2½ ounces)
½ cup chopped green onions
3 cups cooked brown rice
1 cup cooked wild rice
½ cup coarsely chopped toasted hazelnuts
2 tablespoons chopped fresh parsley
• Salt to taste
• Freshly ground black pepper to taste

In a large skillet over medium high heat, melt butter and oil. Sauté mushrooms until golden, about four to five minutes. Add green onions and sauté for about one minute. Add brown and wild rice and stir until hot. Toss with hazelnuts and parsley. Season with salt and pepper to taste.

Brown Rice

2½ cups cold water
1 teaspoon salt
1 cup brown rice

In a medium saucepan, bring water to boil. Add salt and rice and return water to a boil. Cover with a tight-fitting lid and lower heat to simmer. Simmer for 45 minutes to one hour, or until rice is tender. Makes three cups cooked brown rice.

Wild Rice

2 cups cold water
½ teaspoon salt
1 cup wild rice

In a medium saucepan, bring water to boil. Add salt and wild rice and return water to boil. Cover with a tight-fitting lid and lower heat to simmer. Simmer for 45 minutes or until rice is tender. Makes about two cups wild rice.

EASE OF
PREPARATION: 1

PREPARATION TIME:
10 MINUTES

COOKING TIME:
10 MINUTES

YIELD: 6 CUPS

PHOTO: INCLUDED
ON COVER

NOTE: Do not remove lid or stir rice during cooking or gummy rice will result. The cooking time will vary with the amount of moisture in the rice, the altitude, and hardness of the cooking water.

Fettucini with Crab & Lemon Sauce

EASE OF
PREPARATION: 2

PREPARATION TIME:
20 MINUTES

COOKING TIME:
15 MINUTES

YIELD:
4 TO 6 SERVINGS

NOTE: To avoid last
minute hassle and a
drooping hairdo,
pasta may be cooked
several hours in
advance and
refrigerated. Reheat
it by rinsing with hot
water, or by
sprinkling it with
several tablespoons
of cold water and
reheating in
microwave oven.

NOTE: See note on
how to stretch crab
on page 44.

NOTE: See how to
select, clean, and
store mushrooms on
page 20.

This recipe really shines when made with fresh Oregon Dungeness crab.

2 tablespoons butter, divided
¾ cup coarsely chopped toasted hazelnuts
5 ounces fresh mushrooms, sliced
    (about 2 cups sliced)
2 cups Chicken Stock (page 37)
½ cup whipping cream
2 egg yolks
3 tablespoons fresh lemon juice
• Cooked fettucini
1 cup fresh Oregon Dungeness crab meat
2 tablespoons chopped fresh dill weed
    (1 tablespoon dried)
• Salt to taste
• Freshly ground black pepper to taste

Heat one tablespoon butter in large skillet. Add hazelnuts and, over medium heat, toss until nuts are a deep golden color, about two minutes. Remove nuts with a slotted spoon and drain on paper towels.

Heat the remaining butter in the same skillet. Over medium high heat, sauté mushrooms until golden, about four to five minutes. Remove from the pan and reserve. Pour Chicken Stock (page 37) into hot pan and cook, over medium high heat, until reduced by about half. Add cream and again reduce by half. Remove skillet from the heat and quickly whisk egg yolks and lemon juice into sauce. Return to low heat and stir until slightly thickened and temperature reaches 160 degrees.

Add the pasta, crab meat, dill weed, and the reserved hazelnuts and mushrooms. Toss with sauce until ingredients are heated through, adding salt and pepper to taste.

Fettucini

2½ quarts water
2 teaspoons salt
8 ounces fettucini noodles

In a four-quart kettle, bring water to boil. Add salt and fettucini, stir, and cook until just barely tender, about 8 to 10 minutes. Drain and rinse, if desired.

Garnish with lemon slices, dill sprigs, and whole toasted hazelnuts.

LOW-FAT TIP: A lighter version of this recipe can be made by substituting lighter cream and eliminating the egg yolks. Thicken sauce by dissolving two teaspoons cornstarch in ¼ cup Chicken Stock. After reducing stock and cream, whisk into sauce and cook for several minutes or until slightly thickened.

Pasta Nut Carbonara

One of my favorite flavor combinations is bacon and hazelnuts. Both work well with the other ingredients in this recipe.

The original Pasta Carbonara was deliciously loaded with cream and egg yolks. This lighter version has the flavor without the extra fat.

4 slices thick sliced bacon,
   cut in 1 inch pieces
2 cloves garlic, minced
1 small onion, chopped (½ cup)
3 medium ripe tomatoes, peeled, seeded,
   and coarsely chopped (3 cups)
• Cooked spaghetti
¼ cup finely chopped parsley
½ teaspoon salt
• Freshly ground black pepper to taste
½ cup coarsely chopped hazelnuts
½ cup grated parmesan cheese

In a large skillet or microwave, fry bacon until crisp. Drain on paper towels. Pour off all but one tablespoon bacon fat (may use olive oil or vegetable oil if desired) and, over medium heat, sauté garlic and onion for about four minutes, or until softened.

Add tomatoes and stir until heated through.

Add cooked spaghetti, parsley and reserved bacon. Cook until just heated through. Add salt and pepper to taste. Mix in hazelnuts and top with grated parmesan cheese.

Spaghetti
2½ quarts water
2 teaspoons salt
8 ounces spaghetti

In a four-quart kettle, bring water to a boil. Add salt and spaghetti, stir, and cook until just barely tender, about eight to ten minutes. Drain and rinse, if desired.

EASE OF
PREPARATION: 1

PREPARATION TIME:
10 MINUTES

COOKING TIME:
12 MINUTES

YIELD:
4 TO 6 SERVINGS

NOTE: To peel and seed tomatoes, see page 59.

Curried Rice with Hazelnuts

With just a hint of Eastern influence, this dish works well as an accompaniment to poultry and lamb and can also stretch as a main dish with the addition of tiny bits of chicken or fish.

2 tablespoons butter
¼ cup finely chopped green onions
¼ cup finely diced carrots
¼ cup finely diced green pepper
3 cups cooked white rice
¼ cup finely chopped toasted hazelnuts
½ teaspoon curry powder
2 tablespoons minced parsley

In a large skillet, melt butter over medium high heat. Sauté green onions, carrots, and green pepper for several minutes or until just slightly softened. Stir in rice, hazelnuts, curry, and parsley.

NOTE: "Curry" is sort of a catch-all name for different mixtures of spices and peppers used most often in Indian cooking. As each curry powder is different, it is difficult to specify the exact amount that should be used. Therefore, it is best to add about half the amount suggested, and keep adding more until the flavor is right.

NOTE: To cook White Rice, see page 50.

EASE OF
PREPARTION: 1

PREPARATION TIME:
10 MINUTES

COOKING TIME:
5 MINUTES

YIELD: 6 SERVINGS

*H*azelnut Pesto Pasta

EASE OF
PREPARATION: 1

PREPARATION TIME:
10 MINUTES

COOKING TIME:
10 MINUTES

YIELD:
4 TO 6 SERVINGS

DID YOU KNOW . . .
That the hazelnut
shell can be used to
dry-smoke foods,
imparting a buttery,
smoky sweet taste.

*The family will love this quick and flavorful
pasta. Add a few cooked shrimp and turn it into
an instant company dish. The pesto can be
prepared in advance and the remaining
ingredients prepared while the pasta is cooking.*

8 ounces spaghetti, cooked (see page 63)
½ to 1 cup Hazelnut Pesto
2 medium fresh tomatoes, peeled,
    seeded, and diced (see page 59)
• Freshly ground black pepper to taste
½ cup coarsely chopped toasted hazelnuts
• Grated parmesan cheese to taste

Toss hot spaghetti with Hazelnut Pesto
to taste. Mix in tomatoes and a sprinkling
of freshly ground black pepper. Top with
toasted hazelnuts and a sprinkling of
grated parmesan cheese.

Hazelnut Pesto
2 cups packed fresh basil leaves
3 cloves garlic
1 cup grated parmesan cheese
¾ cup finely chopped toasted hazelnuts
½ to ¾ cup olive oil
• Salt to taste
• Freshly ground pepper to taste

Puree basil leaves and garlic in food
processor or blender. Mix in parmesan and
hazelnuts. With machine running, drizzle
in just enough olive oil to make a thin
paste. Season with salt and pepper.
Refrigerate for up to one week, or one
month tightly sealed in freezer.

NOTE: To save on calories, this pesto is a
little thicker than some recipes. If a thinner
consistency is desired, add more oil.

No longer just supporting players in the culinary field, vegetables are now taking their rightful place on the center of the plate. With their vitamins, minerals and protein, hazelnuts and vegetables are definitely a winning team.

Vegetable cookery has my vote for the most improved technique of the past decade. No longer are mushy, overcooked vegetables the norm. No wonder we are eating more of them!

There are two schools of thought on how to cook vegetables.

The first is that in order to retain their color, green vegetables should be cooked in a large amount of water. The preferred method is to bring several quarts of water to a boil, drop in the prepared vegetables, and cover only until water returns to a boil. Cook uncovered for the remainder of the cooking time. This method enhances the natural colors of the vegetables.

The second method calls for vegetables to be cooked in a very small amount of water or steamed in order to retain their Vitamin C. It is up to the cook to choose between the two methods—beauty or practicality. In any event, most green vegetables should be cooked only until tender-crisp, or until they can be just barely pierced with a fork.

Vegetables can be cooked in advance and held overnight, if necessary. In order to retain their bright, fresh color, they should be cooked rapidly and chilled thoroughly. Immediately drain cooked vegetables in a colander and cool with cold running water. Transfer to a bowl of ice water to finish chilling. Drain well, pat dry, and wrap in paper towels. Store in plastic bags in the refrigerator.

To refresh vegetables, quickly re-heat in microwave, or plunge them briefly into boiling water.

Wrap the individual patties in plastic wrap and freeze. There is no need to defrost—they can be heated in a nonstick skillet for a quick, healthy meal. The mixture can also be sautéed and used for tacos, burritos, and more.

2 teaspoons olive oil
1 small onion (½ cup chopped)
1½ cups coarsely chopped mushrooms
1 cup cooked brown rice (See page 61)
1 cup cooked pinto beans, pureed in
    blender or food processor
½ cup toasted bread crumbs
2 ounces (½ cup) grated
    mozzarella cheese
½ cup finely chopped toasted hazelnuts
2 tablespoons chopped parsley
1 teaspoon chopped fresh thyme
    (½ teaspoon dried)
1 egg white, beaten until frothy
½ teaspoon salt
⅛ teaspoon freshly ground black pepper

In a 10 to 12 inch skillet, over medium heat, cook onion in olive oil until it is soft and translucent, about three minutes. Add mushrooms and continue cooking, stirring often, until most of the moisture has evaporated and the mixture is a very dark brown, about five to eight minutes.

Transfer mixture to a three-quart mixing bowl and mix in remaining ingredients; taste and adjust seasonings.

Veggie Nut Burgers

Form six patties, ½ inch thick, between sheets of plastic wrap.

Lightly spray broiler pan with nonstick vegetable oil spray. Place patties on pan and lightly brush tops with vegetable oil or non-stick vegetable oil spray. Broil for two minutes on each side, or until top is slightly browned.

Serve on a fresh bun with all your favorite burger accompaniments.

NOTE: If mixture is too soft to hold together, add several additional table-spoons of bread crumbs.

TIP: When chopped mushrooms must be cooked almost dry, the process can be speeded up by placing them in the center of a lightweight kitchen towel. Bring the towel up and over the mushrooms and twist to form a tight pack. Keep twisting and squeezing until liquid no longer drips from the towel. It is surprising how much liquid can be drawn.

EASE OF PREPARATION: 1

PREPARATION TIME: 15 MINUTES

COOKING TIME: 12 TO 15 MINUTES

TO COOK INGREDIENTS: 15 MINUTES

ACTUAL COOKING TIME: 4 TO 5 MINUTES

YIELD: 6 BURGERS

PHOTO - BURGER: PAGE 126
PHOTO - BUN: PAGE 74

NOTE: See how to select, clean, and store mushrooms on page 20.

Fresh Vegetables with Herbs & Nuts

EASE OF
PREPARATION: 1

PREPARATION TIME:
15 MINUTES,
DEPENDING UPON
CHOICE OF
VEGETABLES

COOKING TIME:
20 MINUTES,
DEPENDING UPON
CHOICE OF
VEGETABLES

YIELD:
4 TO 6 SERVINGS

PHOTO: PAGE 66

This is a simple dish that brings out the freshness of the vegetables.

1½ pounds seasonal fresh vegetables,
    peeled and cut in serving size pieces
    (asparagus, carrots, yellow squash,
    green beans, cauliflower, etc.)
¼ cup melted butter
1 clove garlic, minced
2 teaspoons chopped fresh dill weed
    (1 teaspoon dried)
½ teaspoon chopped fresh thyme
    (¼ teaspoon dried)
¼ cup grated parmesan cheese
¼ finely chopped toasted hazelnuts

Steam or boil vegetables separately until tender-crisp.

Mix together butter, garlic, and herbs. Pour over the vegetables. Sprinkle with parmesan cheese and hazelnuts.

LOW FAT TIP: The butter, parmesan, and nuts can be reduced to approximately one tablespoon each and still preserve a hint of the flavors.

NOTE: Use the best parmesan available, such as Parmigiano Reggiano. In the long run, it will save both calories and money, as the flavor is so intense you will use less.

Green Beans with Hazelnut Garnish

EASE OF
PREPARATION: 1

PREPARATION TIME:
8 MINUTES

COOKING TIME:
7 MINUTES

YIELD:
4 TO 6 SERVINGS

Use only fresh beans that snap when they are broken.

1½ pounds whole fresh green beans
• 2 quarts cold water
1 teaspoon salt
1 tablespoon hazelnut oil
    (see Glossary, pages 123-124)
⅓ cup coarsely chopped toasted hazelnuts
• Freshly ground black pepper to taste

Wash and sort green beans. Remove stem ends, but leave tips if desired.

In a four-quart covered saucepan, bring water and salt to boil.

Add green beans, cover just until water comes back to a boil.

Remove cover and cook for about five minutes, or just until tender. Drain, and pat off any excess moisture.

Heat hazelnut oil in large skillet. Drop the beans in the hot oil and stir for about one minute just to coat lightly with the oil. Add the hazelnuts and toss until well mixed.

Pour beans onto serving platter and top with freshly ground black pepper.

New Potatoes with Hazelnuts & Cheese

Susan Mahony and her husband Phil are hazelnut growers, so they always have plenty on hand to try new recipes. This is one of their favorites.

1½ pounds tiny new Yukon Gold or
    Red potatoes, unpeeled
• Water
1 teaspoon salt
1 tablespoon butter
3 cloves roasted garlic (2 teaspoons)
¼ cup grated Parmesan cheese
¼ cup finely chopped toasted hazelnuts

❦

Wash potatoes and peel a ¼-inch strip around the center of each to prevent bursting while cooking. Place in a two-quart saucepan with salt and water to cover. Cover pan, bring to boil. Reduce heat to low and simmer until fork tender, about 15 minutes. Drain.

Melt butter in 10 to 12 inch skillet. Add garlic and mix into a paste with the butter.

Add potatoes to pan and toss to coat with butter and garlic. Sprinkle with parmesan cheese and hazelnuts, and serve.

Roasted Garlic

With a sharp knife cut about ½ inch off the top of a garlic bulb. Place in a small oven proof dish lined with aluminum foil. Drizzle olive oil over the cut surface, and bake in a 350-degree oven until garlic is very soft, about 30 to 45 minutes, depending on the size and freshness of the garlic.

Cool slightly and squeeze softened garlic out of the skins. Will keep in refrigerator, tightly covered, for several days.

EASE OF
PREPARATION: 1

PREPARATION TIME:
10 MINUTES

COOKING TIME:
15 TO 20 MINUTES

YIELD:
4 TO 6 SERVINGS

Mashed Potatoes with Onions & Hazelnuts

Plain old "smashed potatoes" are hard to beat, but this treatment is a nice change.

1½ to 2 pounds Yukon Gold or
    Russet potatoes
• Water
2 teaspoons salt
3 tablespoons butter, divided
1 small onion, sliced (1 cup)
1 teaspoon granulated sugar
½ cup milk, or as needed
¼ cup, plus 2 tablespoons coarsely
    chopped toasted hazelnuts
• Freshly ground black pepper

❦

Peel potatoes and cut into quarters. Place in three to four quart saucepan and cover with water. Add salt, cover, and cook until potatoes can be easily pierced with a fork, approximately 15 to 20 minutes. Drain well.

While potatoes are cooking, melt one tablespoon butter in a small skillet. Add onion and sauté until a deep golden color, adding sugar during the last several minutes of cooking to hasten browning. Keep warm.

Break up potatoes with a potato masher or fork. Add half of the milk and the remaining two tablespoons butter and beat with electric mixer or potato masher. Add remaining milk, a little at a time, until mixture is light and fluffy. Fold in ¼ cup hazelnuts. Season with salt and freshly ground black pepper to taste.

To serve, spoon potatoes into serving bowl and top with sautéed onions, and sprinkle with remaining hazelnuts.

EASE OF
PREPARATION: 1

PREPARATION TIME:
15 MINUTES

COOKING TIME:
20 MINUTES

YIELD:
4 TO 6 SERVINGS

Brussels Sprouts with Hazelnuts & Bacon

Brussels sprouts have gotten a bad rap as the vegetable most often used to threaten children into civilized behavior. If you are still harboring the bitter taste of childhood, this recipe may sweeten those biting memories.

1½ pounds Brussels sprouts
2 quarts cold water
1 teaspoon salt
2 pieces thick sliced bacon,
   diced in ½ inch pieces
⅓ cup coarsely chopped toasted hazelnuts

Prepare the Brussels sprouts by washing and trimming off the stem end even with the first leaves. Pull off any wilted leaves. Make a ¼-inch-deep X slash on the cut end.

In a four-quart covered saucepan, bring water and salt to boil. Add the prepared Brussels sprouts and cover just until the water returns to a boil. Uncover and cook for about five minutes or until Brussels sprouts can be pierced easily with the tip of a knife. Drain.

In the meantime, fry the bacon until crisp in a 10 to 12 inch skillet. Pour off all but one tablespoon of the bacon drippings. Add the Brussels sprouts, toss to coat well with the bacon drippings, and continue cooking for several minutes until the sprouts are slightly browned. Stir in chopped hazelnuts and serve.

NOTE: Choose Brussels sprouts that are firm and green. Select sprouts of similar size so that they cook evenly.

Stuffed Tomatoes

This stuffing works equally well with other vegetables—acorn squash, zucchini, and mushroom caps to name a few.

1 tablespoon olive oil
¼ cup finely chopped onion
1 cup finely chopped mushrooms
½ cup toasted bread crumbs
½ cup grated parmesan cheese
½ cup medium chopped toasted hazelnuts
2 teaspoons fresh chopped basil
    (½ teaspoon dried)
½ teaspoon salt
Several grinds black pepper
2 tablespoons melted butter
4 medium fresh tomatoes

Heat oil in small skillet. Sauté onion until softened, about four minutes. Add mushrooms and continue cooking until dark brown, about five minutes. Cool for several minutes and place in small mixing bowl. Add remaining ingredients, in order given. Mix well.

Slice tomatoes in half horizontally. Remove the seeds. (See How to Seed a Tomato, page 59), and slice a thin slice off the bottoms so they will stand upright.

Fill the cavity with stuffing, mounding slightly in the center. Place on broiler pan and bake in 350-degree oven just until the tomatoes are heated through. Heat broiler. Place tomatoes about three inches from the heat and broil just until topping is browned, about one to two minutes.

NOTE: Very firm vegetables like winter squash should be pre-cooked slightly before stuffing.

This casserole-style dish is a natural at Thanksgiving, or for any poultry dinner. The sweet potato portion can be made a day in advance and the cranberries added just before popping into the oven.

2 pounds fresh sweet potatoes
¼ cup cream
2 tablespoons orange juice concentrate
2 tablespoons hazelnut liqueur
    (such as Frangelico)
1 teaspoon orange zest
    (See Glossary, pages 123-124)
3 large eggs
½ cup milk, or as needed
¾ cup finely chopped, toasted hazelnuts
• Cranberry sauce
¼ cup parmesan cheese

Cook sweet potatoes in simmering water until tender, about 20 minutes. Drain and cool until lukewarm; peel. Whip peeled potatoes with electric mixer, adding cream, orange juice concentrate, hazelnut liqueur, orange zest, and eggs, one at a time, and enough milk to make a smooth, but not runny, puree. Stir in ½ cup finely chopped, toasted hazelnuts.

Generously spray an 8 x 12 x 2 inch baking dish with non-stick spray. Spread sweet potatoes in the baking dish, and with a knife, make a ¾ inch "ditch" dividing the sweet potatoes in half, both cross-wise and length-wise.

Gratin of Sweet Potatoes, Hazelnuts, & Cranberries

Spoon the sauce in the space between the sweet potatoes. Sprinkle sweet potatoes with parmesan and the remaining toasted hazelnuts. Bake in a 350-degree oven until just heated through, about ten minutes.

Cranberry Sauce
1 12-ounce package fresh cranberries
1 cup orange juice
¾ cup sugar, or to taste
1 whole orange, peeled

Rinse and sort through cranberries, discarding any that are soft or blemished. Place in a two-quart saucepan with orange juice and sugar. Bring to a boil, reduce heat, and simmer until the cranberries are soft, about ten minutes, stirring occasionally. Cut orange into ½-inch pieces and add to cranberries during the last several minutes of cooking. Taste, adjust sweetener, and cool.

EASE OF
PREPARATION: 2

PREPARATION TIME:
30 MINUTES

COOKING AND
BAKING TIME:
30 TO 40 MINUTES

YIELD:
8 TO 10 SERVINGS

NOTE: Fresh cranberries are almost impossible to get when not in season, so it is a good idea to purchase a few extra bags during the holidays and keep them in the freezer. In a pinch, canned whole cranberry sauce can be used. Add a diced orange and a little orange zest to give it a fresher flavor.

Vegetable Strudel

NOTE: For tips on working with Phyllo dough, see pages 14 and 15.

○ ○ ○

EASE OF
PREPARATION: 3

PREPARATION TIME:
30 MINUTES

COOKING TIME:
10 MINUTES

BAKING TIME:
20 MINUTES

YIELD:
2 ROLLS, 4 TO 6
SERVINGS EACH

NOTE: See how to select, clean, and store mushrooms on page 20.

Don't let the length of the recipe alarm you. It goes together easily and can be done ahead in several steps. The vegetables can be prepared and held overnight, and the finished rolls will keep in the refrigerator for several hours. It can also be frozen and reheated in a 375-degree oven.

The recipe can be cut in half, but while you are at it, why not make two?

2 tablespoons olive oil
1 pound mushrooms, cleaned and sliced
• Salt to taste
• Freshly ground black pepper to taste
½ cup chopped green onions
8 ounces chopped fresh spinach,
    medium chopped
2 carrots, peeled and coarsely grated
8 sheets Phyllo (fillo) dough, thawed
½ cup (approximate) clarified, unsalted
    butter, melted
    (See Glossary, pages 123-124)
½ cup finely ground toasted hazelnuts
½ cup grated parmesan cheese

○

Melt one tablespoon oil in a large skillet. Over high heat sauté mushrooms until golden brown, about five minutes, stirring often. Season with salt and pepper to taste. Remove from skillet and drain on paper towels; cool.

Heat remaining oil in the same skillet. Over medium high heat, sauté green onions and spinach for about two minutes. Season with salt and pepper. Drain on paper towels until cool. Pat off excess moisture.

In same skillet toss grated carrots for about one minute, adding a little additional oil if needed. Drain on paper towels until cool. Heat oven to 375 degrees.

Brush one sheet of Phyllo lightly with melted butter. Sprinkle with about one tablespoon finely chopped hazelnuts and one tablespoon parmesan cheese. Layer with three additional sheets, repeating with butter, hazelnuts, and parmesan.

On the short end of the dough, place half of the spinach mixture in a two-inch-wide strip, one inch from the bottom and the sides. Top with half of the mushrooms and half of the carrots. Fold the long, one-inch edges over the filling and all the way up the sides of the dough. Fold the bottom edge up over the filling. Carefully roll the dough around the filling so that you end up with carrots on top and the seam on the bottom. Don't roll it too tightly, or the filling will cook out when baked.

Repeat with remaining ingredients to make two rolls.

Brush rolls with melted butter. Sprinkle with parmesan and hazelnuts. With a sharp knife, score the top of the roll in serving-size pieces, cutting almost all the way through the pastry. Bake in a 375-degree oven until golden, approximately 20 minutes. Let stand several minutes before slicing. Serve with Mustard/Lime Sauce.

Mustard/Lime Sauce
½ cup mayonnaise
2 to 3 tablespoons fresh lime juice
2 teaspoons dijon mustard
2 tablespoons cream

○

Mix all ingredients until smooth. Refrigerate.

There is something homey and satisfying about baking yeast breads. Maybe it is the perfume that wafts throughout the house. Maybe it is the wonder of watching this lump of dough come alive—literally—and maybe it is the pleasure of creating something that mystifies so many people.

The secret to bread baking is that it is really pretty easy. Yeast, water and flour are all it takes. As with any discipline, however, an understanding of ingredients and techniques streamline the process.

For years home bakers made bread entirely by hand, and many still do. Yeast and liquids were stirred together and flour was added, a little at a time, until the dough was too stiff to stir. It was then placed on a floured surface and kneaded by hand until it was smooth and elastic. Then came electric mixers. They were helpful in getting the first part of the dough mixed together, but were not powerful enough to mix all of the flour. There was still a lot of hand work.

With the advent of heavy duty mixers, it all could be done by machine. Now with food processors and bread machines, bread making is certainly faster and easier. Whether is it better, though, is debatable. There is still a lot to be said for the therapeutic value of hand kneading.

My favorite tool, however, is the food processor. Although most yeast bread recipes are designed for a heavy-duty upright mixer, as this is the standard method to which most people are accustomed, they can be converted for use in the processor. Just make sure your machine is large and powerful enough to handle the recipe. Check with the instruction book for capacity, choice of blades, etc.

The standard food processor method is to first proof the yeast, along with a little bit of sugar, in the liquid in a measuring cup. Place the dry ingredients in the work bowl, fitted with the proper blade, and with the machine running, pour the yeast and liquids in a slow, steady stream, just fast enough for the flour to absorb the liquid. If the dough is too dry, add more liquid, one teaspoon at a time. If the dough is too soft, add flour, one tablespoon at a time. Knead for 30 to 90 seconds, depending upon the type of dough. Place in oiled bowl, cover, let rise, and proceed with the recipe.

Often food processor recipes will call for a small amount of warm water (¼ cup) in which to proof the yeast, and specify that remaining liquid be cold. This is because the kneading process warms the dough and using cold water reduces the risk of over-kneading and possibly killing the yeast.

See page 81 for tips on yeast bread baking.

*Moist and chewy, with the added texture
of cracked wheat and hazelnuts, this bread
is excellent for sandwiches and toast. It also
freezes well.*

Hazelnut Cracked Wheat Bread

½ cup plus 2 tablespoons cracked wheat
• Boiling water
2 tablespoons or 2 packages
    (¼ ounce each) active dry yeast
2 cups warm water, 105 to 115 degrees
¼ cup honey
¼ cup softened butter
2 teaspoons salt
3½ cups unbleached white flour
2½ cups whole wheat flour
¾ cup plus 2 tablespoons coarsely
    chopped toasted hazelnuts

Pour boiling water over ½ cup cracked
wheat. Let stand for about three minutes.
Drain and press out excess water.

Stir yeast, warm water and honey
together in a large bowl. Let stand until
foamy, about three minutes. Add butter,
salt, and two cups of the white flour. With
electric mixer or by hand, beat until the
consistency of thick cake batter, about two
minutes. Gradually mix in remaining flours
and soaked cracked wheat. With heavy
duty mixer, or by hand, knead until dough
is smooth and elastic.

Place in greased bowl, turn to coat the
entire ball, cover with a dampened kitchen
towel, and let rise until doubled in bulk,
about 45 minutes. Punch down and turn
out onto lightly floured surface. Sprinkle
dough with ½ cup hazelnuts. Gently knead
the nuts into the dough.

Divide dough into two pieces. Form the
dough into two discs that are about eight
inches in diameter and one inch thick.
Place on greased baking sheets. Cover with
oiled plastic wrap, and let rise until a slight
indentation remains when lightly pressed
with fingertips, about 45 minutes.

Shortly before baking time, position a
baking rack in the center of the oven and
heat the oven to 375 degrees. Brush the
tops of the loaves with Egg Yolk Glaze
(page 85) and sprinkle with remaining
cracked wheat and hazelnuts. Bake on the
center rack of a 375-degree oven for about
30 to 35 minutes, or until the tops are
golden and the internal temperature is 185
to 190 degrees. Cool on racks.

EASE OF
PREPARATION: 3

PREPARATION AND
SHAPING TIME:
25 MINUTES

RISING TIME:
1 HOUR, 30 MINUTES

BAKING TIME:
35 MINUTES

YIELD:
2 1½ POUND LOAVES

PHOTO INCLUDED
ON FRONT COVER

Cheese, Onion, & Hazelnut Twist

FOR PHOTO:
SEE PAGE 74

EASE OF
PREPARATION: 3

PREPARATION AND
SHAPING TIME:
30 MINUTES

RISING TIME:
1 HOUR, 30 MINUTES

BAKING TIME:
30 MINUTES

YIELD: 1 LOAF

Try this hearty bread as an accompaniment to a soup or salad lunch. Gruyere cheese would be my first choice, but other flavorful Swiss cheeses are good too. Do not overbake, or the filling may bake out.

Dough

1 tablespoon or 1 package (¼ ounce)
    active dry yeast
1 cup warm water, 105 to 115 degrees
1 tablespoon granulated sugar
¼ cup softened butter
1 teaspoon salt
2 cups unbleached white flour
1 cup whole wheat flour

Stir yeast, warm water and sugar together in a large bowl. Let stand until foamy, about three minutes. Add butter, salt, and 1¼ cups of the white flour. With electric mixer, or by hand, beat until the consistency of thick cake batter, about two minutes. Gradually mix in remaining flours. With heavy duty mixer, or by hand, knead until dough is smooth and elastic.

Place in greased bowl, turn to coat the entire ball, cover with dampened kitchen towel, and let rise until doubled in bulk, about 45 minutes.

While dough is rising prepare filling.

Turn dough out onto a lightly floured surface. Press out air bubbles and divide into two pieces. Press into two rectangles about 4 x 14 inches. Spread half of the filling down the center of each piece, in a strip 1½ inches wide and about 1 inch thick. Form two ropes by bringing the sides of the dough up to encase the filling; pinch together. Place the seam side down on the counter and gently roll with fingertips to smooth the seam out. The finished length of the ropes should be about 18 inches long.

Place the two pieces parallel to each other on a lightly greased baking sheet, seam side down. Pinch the two pieces together on one end, tuck under, and gently twist the ropes, one over the other, always keeping the seam side down. Pinch the end piece together and tuck under.

Cover the twist with oiled plastic wrap and let rise until a slight indentation remains when lightly pressed with finger tip, about 30 to 45 minutes. Shortly before baking time, position a baking rack in the center of the oven and heat the oven to 375 degrees. Brush the top of the loaf with Egg Yolk Glaze (page 85).

Bake on the center rack of a 375-degree oven for 30 minutes or until golden. Cool on racks.

Cheese-Onion Filling

2 teaspoons olive oil
1 cup chopped onion (1 medium)
4 ounces cream cheese, softened
1 cup shredded Gruyere (Swiss) cheese
    (3 ounces)
½ cup finely chopped toasted hazelnuts

Heat olive oil in small skillet. Sauté onion over medium heat until it is soft and golden, about five minutes, stirring often; cool. In small bowl mix together cream cheese, Gruyere cheese, toasted hazelnuts and reserved onions.

Whole Wheat Hazelnut Dinner Rolls

These rolls can be shaped into balls, twists, or knots, as well as hamburger buns and bread sticks.

1 tablespoon or 1 package (¼ ounce) active dry yeast

¾ cup warm water, 105 to 115 degrees

2 tablespoons granulated sugar

¼ cup instant dry milk

¼ cup (½ stick) softened butter

2 large eggs

1 teaspoon salt

2 cups unbleached white flour

1¼ cup whole wheat flour

1 cup finely chopped toasted hazelnuts

Stir yeast, warm water, and sugar together in a large bowl. Let stand until foamy, about three minutes. Add dry milk, butter, eggs, salt and 1½ cups of the white flour. With electric mixer, or by hand, beat until the consistency of thick cake batter, approximately two minutes. Gradually mix in remaining flours and hazelnuts. With heavy duty mixer, or by hand, knead until dough is smooth and elastic.

Place in a greased bowl, turn to coat the entire ball, cover with a dampened kitchen towel, and let rise until doubled in bulk, about 60 to 90 minutes. Punch down and turn out onto lightly floured surface. Form into desired shapes and place several inches apart on greased baking sheet. Cover with oiled plastic wrap and let rise until a slight indentation remains when lightly pressed with finger tips, about 45 to 60 minutes. Shortly before baking time, position a baking rack in the center of the oven and heat the oven to 375 degrees.

Brush with Egg Yolk Glaze (page 85) taking care not to let any drip onto baking sheet. Bake on the center rack of a 375-degree oven for about 15 to 18 minutes, depending upon size, or until the tops are golden. Cool on racks.

EASE OF
PREPARATION: 3

PREPARATION AND
SHAPING TIME:
35 MINUTES

RISING TIME:
1 TO 2 HOURS

BAKING TIME:
15 TO 18 MINUTES

YIELD:
3 TO 4 DOZEN,
DEPENDING ON SIZE

FOR PHOTOS:
SEE PAGE 74
& PAGE 126

NOTE: Because this dough contains more butter and eggs than basic yeast doughs, it will take longer to rise.

Caramelized Onion Focaccia

EASE OF
PREPARATION: 2

PREPARATION AND
SHAPING TIME:
25 MINUTES

RISING TIME:
1 HOUR, 30 MINUTES

BAKING TIME:
18 TO 20 MINUTES

YIELD:
1 12-INCH FOCACCIA

PHOTO:
SEE PAGE 74

No one can resist the aroma of onion bread. This crisp Focaccia should be eaten when it is freshly made. It can be frozen and reheated in the oven; however, reheating in the microwave will make it soft and tough. It can also be sliced horizontally for sandwiches.

1 tablespoon or package (¼ ounce)
   active dry yeast
1 cup warm water, 105 to 115 degrees
3 teaspoons granulated sugar, divided
1 teaspoon salt
3 tablespoons olive oil, divided
3 cups unbleached white flour
1 medium onion (1½ cups) thinly sliced
¼ cup coarsely chopped toasted hazelnuts
2 teaspoons fresh rosemary leaves
   (1 teaspoon dried)
½ teaspoon coarse salt for topping
¼ cup coarsely chopped toasted hazelnuts

Stir yeast, warm water and two teaspoons sugar together in a large bowl. Let stand until foamy, about three minutes. Add one teaspoon salt, one tablespoon olive oil and 1½ cups flour. With electric mixer, or by hand, beat until the dough is the consistency of thick cake batter, approximately two minutes.

Gradually mix in the remaining flour until a firm dough is formed. With heavy duty mixer, or by hand, knead until the dough is smooth and elastic.

Place in a greased bowl, turn to coat the entire ball, cover with a dampened kitchen towel, and let rise until doubled in bulk, about 45 minutes.

While the dough is rising, in a medium skillet, heat two teaspoons olive oil and sauté onions over medium heat until they are golden, about five minutes. To help brown, sprinkle with the remaining teaspoon of sugar during the last few minutes of cooking. Cool.

Turn the dough out onto a lightly floured surface. Punch down and form into a 12-inch round. Place on a 12-inch pizza-type pan that has been brushed with olive oil, cover with oiled plastic wrap, and let rise until almost doubled, about 30 minutes. Shortly before baking time, position a baking rack in the center of the oven and heat the oven to 425 degrees.

Press fingers into the risen dough, leaving indentations to catch some of the oil and toppings. Brush with olive oil, spread onions over the dough, sprinkle with rosemary, coarse salt, and the toasted hazelnuts. Bake on center rack of a 425-degree oven for about 18 to 20 minutes, or until golden. Cool on rack.

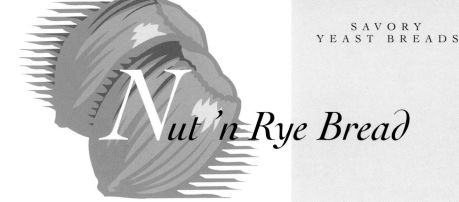

Nut 'n Rye Bread

This dense, dark bread is a good background for cheese spreads and fillings. It is especially good with the Smoked Salmon Pâté on page 22. It can also be formed into two small baguettes and used as cocktail rye.

1 tablespoon or 1 package (¼ ounce)
    active dry yeast
1 cup warm water, 105 to 115 degrees
2 tablespoons dark molasses
2 tablespoons vegetable oil
1 teaspoon salt
2 cups unbleached white flour
3 tablespoons Dutch process cocoa
    (See Glossary, pages 123-124)
1 cup rye flour
½ cup, plus 1 tablespoon,
    coarsely chopped toasted hazelnuts

Stir yeast, warm water, and molasses together in a large bowl. Let stand until foamy, about three minutes. Add vegetable oil, salt, and 1½ cups of the white flour. With electric mixer, or by hand, beat until the consistency of thick cake batter, about two minutes. Gradually mix in cocoa and the remaining flours until a firm dough is formed. With a heavy duty mixer or by hand, knead until the dough is smooth and elastic.

Place in a greased bowl, turn to coat the entire ball, cover with a dampened kitchen towel, and let rise until doubled in bulk, about 60 minutes. Punch down and turn out onto lightly floured surface. Press out air bubbles, knead in ½ cup hazelnuts, and form into a round loaf, about eight inches in diameter. Place on greased baking sheet. Cover with oiled plastic wrap and let rise until a slight indentation remains when lightly touched with finger tips, about 45 minutes. Shortly before baking time, position a baking rack in the center of the oven and heat the oven to 375 degrees.

Brush with Egg Yolk Glaze (page 85) taking care not to let any drip onto the baking sheet. Sprinkle with the remaining one tablespoon coarsely chopped hazelnuts, make several diagonal slits on top, and bake on center rack of a 375-degree oven for about 30 minutes, or until the internal temperature is 185 to 190 degrees. Cool on rack.

EASE OF
PREPARATION: 3

PREPARATION AND
SHAPING TIME:
20 MINUTES

RISING TIME:
1 HOUR, 45 MINUTES

BAKING TIME:
30 MINUTES

YIELD:
1 - 1¼ POUND LOAF

PHOTO:
SEE PAGE 74

Chilies & Cheese Batter Bread

EASE OF
PREPARATION: 1

PREPARATION AND
SHAPING TIME:
10 MINUTES

RISING TIME:
45 MINUTES

BAKING TIME:
25 MINUTES

SPECIAL
EQUIPMENT:
11 X 7 GLASS BAKING
PAN

YIELD: 8 SERVINGS

DID YOU KNOW . . .
That hazelnut shells
can be used in
landscaping as a
mulch or ground
cover.

Very easy to prepare, this batter bread has an unexpected kick. Excellent with Mexican foods, or with a soup and salad lunch.

1 tablespoon or 1 package ($\frac{1}{4}$ ounce)
   active dry yeast
$\frac{1}{4}$ cup warm water, 105 to 115 degrees
2 teaspoons granulated sugar
$\frac{3}{4}$ cup warm milk, 105-115 degrees
$\frac{1}{4}$ cup softened butter
1 teaspoon salt
$\frac{1}{2}$ teaspoon hot pepper sauce
1$\frac{1}{2}$ cup unbleached white flour
$\frac{1}{2}$ cup yellow cornmeal
2 tablespoons drained green chilies
3 ounces Monterey Jack cheese, grated
   (1 cup)
2 ounces cheddar cheese, grated
   ($\frac{1}{2}$ to $\frac{3}{4}$ cup)
$\frac{1}{2}$ cup medium chopped toasted hazelnuts

Stir yeast, warm water, and sugar together in a large bowl. Let stand until foamy, about three minutes. Add warm milk, butter, salt, hot pepper sauce, and one cup of the white flour.

With mixer, or by hand, beat until the consistency of thick cake batter, about two minutes. Gradually mix in cornmeal and remaining flour. Gently stir in green chilies, $\frac{1}{2}$ cup each of the cheeses, and half of the hazelnuts.

Spray an 11 x 7 inch glass baking pan with nonstick vegetable spray. Spoon dough into the pan, and with fingertips, spread batter evenly. Cover with an oiled plastic wrap and let rise for about 30 minutes, or until it is puffed. Shortly before baking time, position a baking rack in the center of the oven and heat the oven to 375 degrees.

Sprinkle with remaining cheese and hazelnuts and bake on the center rack of a 375-degree oven for 25 minutes, or until puffed and golden. Cool slightly, cut in squares and serve.

Tips for successful bread making: Perfectly kneaded dough is smooth, elastic, and ready for the first rising. Spray a bowl about four times larger than the dough ball with nonstick vegetable spray, or brush with vegetable oil. Place dough in the bowl and turn so both sides are lightly coated with oil. Cover with a barely damp kitchen towel or oiled plastic wrap, so the dough does not stick to the cover. Let rise in a draft-free, warm (75 to 80 degrees is optimum) area until doubled in bulk. The microwave method also works well. Place a cup of water in the microwave and heat to boiling. Place the bowl in the oven with the hot water, and let rise.

There are various conditions that affect rising time: temperature of the kitchen, type of flour, type and amount of yeast, amount of sugar, butter, and eggs. Also, doughs made in the food processor will tend to rise more rapidly because the kneading action of the machine warms the dough.

As dough rises, gas bubbles expand and are trapped by gluten strands in the flour, causing the dough to swell and lighten. When it has about doubled in bulk, you should be able to press a finger several inches into the dough and leave indentation when it is withdrawn. The dough can be turned out and shaped at this point, or it can be punched down for a second rising. Although it is not crucial (my recipes call just for one rising) letting it rise for a second time does develop good flavor.

Generally, a second rising is faster than the first time, and care must be taken not to let the dough over-rise. A slight indentation should remain when lightly touched with a finger tip. If it springs back too quickly, it needs more rising time. If a crater remains without any back-spring—oops—it has risen all it is going to; it will not have the "oomph" to rise any more in the oven. In fact it may deflate. If this happens, a basic loaf can be punched down, re-shaped and tried again, and sometimes again. With gooey fillings, however, it is best to get it right the first time!

Oiled plastic wrap is excellent for covering shaped loaves so they do not dry out. If they dry, they will not rise properly in the oven and may "bolt" from the sides because the gas bubbles cannot penetrate the dried dough. Simply tear off a sheet of plastic wrap, lay it on counter, and spray the top side with nonstick vegetable spray. Flip the sheet over on top of the loaf, and dough will not stick to the cover.

How to tell when it is done: When you can smell the fresh baked bread, when the top is golden, the under side firm and dry, and when the bread sounds hollow when tapped on the bottom, the loaf is very likely done. I must admit, however, that I am not too good at the tapping sounds. I rely on the thermometer. Inserted into the center of the loaf, an accurate, instant-read thermometer should read between 185 and 190 degrees when the loaf is baked to perfection.

Hazelnut Swirl Loaf

Betsy Oppenneer, a master bread baker and Certified Culinary Professional, has provided this recipe. She sells wonderful and unusual breads at Escapades, her shop in Roswell, Georgia. She authored The Bread Book, *an outstanding collection of recipes and techniques for anyone who loves to make yeast breads.*

The Hazelnut Swirl Loaf is wonderful for toast; however, it really shines in a scrumptious sandwich with thinly sliced ham, lettuce, sprouts, mayonnaise, and a little chutney. It is equally good rolled and shaped like a cinnamon roll with the hazelnut filling then lightly drizzled with a confectioner's sugar icing.

Dough

2 scant tablespoons or 2 packages
    (¼ ounce each) active dry yeast
½ cup warm water,
    about (105 to 115 degrees)
1½ cups warm milk
    (about 105 to 115 degrees)
¼ cup honey
¼ cup butter, room temperature
2 large eggs, lightly beaten
2 teaspoons salt
6 to 7 cups unbleached white flour

In a large bowl, stir the yeast into the water to soften. Add milk, honey, butter, eggs, salt, and two cups of the flour to the yeast mixture. Beat vigorously for two minutes.

Gradually add flour, ¼ cup at a time, until the dough begins to pull away from the side of the bowl. Turn the dough out onto a lightly floured work surface. Knead, adding flour a little at a time, until you have a smooth, elastic dough.

Place the dough into an oiled bowl. Turn to coat the entire ball of dough with oil. Cover with a tightly woven towel and let rise until doubled, about one hour.

Turn the dough out onto lightly oiled work surface. Divide in half and roll each half into an 18 x 12 inch rectangle. Spread each rectangle with half of the filling. Roll the dough, from the short end, into an eight-inch roll. Place each roll, seam side down, into a well-greased 8½ x 4¼ inch loaf pan. Cover with a towel and let rise until almost doubled, about 45 minutes.

While the dough is rising, heat the oven to 375 degrees. Bake for 30 minutes, or until the internal temperature reaches 190 degrees. Immediately remove from the pan and cool on a rack to prevent the crust from becoming soggy.

Hazelnut Filling

½ cup cream cheese, room temperature
½ cup light brown sugar
½ teaspoon ground mace
1½ cups finely ground toasted hazelnuts

In a small bowl, mix cream cheese, brown sugar, and mace until smooth. Fold in nuts. Set filling aside.

EASE OF
PREPARATION: 3

PREPARATION TIME:
30 MINUTES

RISING TIME:
1 HOUR, 45 MINUTES

BAKING TIME:
30 MINUTES

YIELD: 2 LOAVES

Toasted Hazelnut Grand Marnier Star

PHOTO: PAGE 82

EASE OF
PREPARATION: 4

PREPARATION AND
SHAPING TIME:
45 MINUTES

CHILLING TIME:
AT LEAST 6 HOURS.

BAKING TIME:
25 MINUTES

YIELD:
2 - 12 INCH ROUND
PASTRIES

The dough for this pastry is quite soft, so it should be very cold when handled. Refrigerate any dough you are not using. It is also helpful to refrigerate the bottom round while working on the top. The recipe makes two pastries. Serve one and freeze the other.

1½ tablespoons or 1½ packages
    (¼ ounce each) active dry yeast
1 cup warm water, 105 to 115 degrees
¼ cup granulated sugar, divided
½ cup butter, softened
¼ cup nonfat dry milk
3 large eggs
1 teaspoon salt
4 cups unbleached white flour

Stir yeast, warm water, and two tablespoons sugar together in a large mixing bowl. Let stand until foamy, about three minutes. Mix in butter, dry milk, eggs, salt, and the remaining sugar. Add 1½ cups of the flour and beat with electric mixer until the consistency of thick cake batter, about two minutes. Gradually mix in remaining flour. With a heavy duty mixer, or by hand, knead until the dough is smooth and elastic.

Place in a greased bowl, turn to coat the entire ball, cover with a dampened kitchen towel, and refrigerate overnight, or for about six hours.

Punch dough down, turn out on to lightly floured surface, and divide into four equal parts. Refrigerate dough that is not being used. Roll one piece of dough into a 11½-inch circle. Place in the center of a greased 12-inch pizza-type pan.

Spread half of the filling on the pastry to within ½ inch of the outer edge. Lightly brush edge with cold water.

Roll another piece of dough into a 11½-inch circle and place on top of the filling. Gently press edges together. Using a two-inch biscuit cutter, make an outline of the circle in the center of the dough. With scissors, make six snips to form a six-pointed star, starting in the center of the pastry and cutting to the outline of the circle. Lay the points open to expose the filling. Sprinkle one tablespoon chopped, toasted hazelnuts over the exposed filling.

With a knife or a pizza cutter, cut pie shaped wedges, starting one inch from the edge of the exposed filling, cutting to the outer edge of the pastry. Wedges should be ½ inch wide at the center and 1½ inches wide at the outside edge. Give each wedge a double twist, forming a starburst pattern.

Repeat with remaining dough, making two pastries. Cover with an oiled plastic wrap and let rise until a slight indentation remains when lightly pressed with finger-tips, about 45 minutes. Shortly before baking, position a baking rack in the center of the oven and heat the oven to 350 degrees.

Brush loaves with Egg Yolk Glaze and bake on the center rack of a 350-degree oven until golden, about 20 to 25 minutes. Cool on rack and drizzle with Orange Glaze.

Filling

Prepare filling just before rolling dough.
6 ounces dried apricots (1 cup)
1 cup brown sugar
8 ounces cream cheese, softened
2 tablespoons Grand Marnier liqueur
½ cup, plus 1 tablespoon,
    finely chopped toasted hazelnuts

❧

Soak apricots in boiling water until softened, about five minutes. Drain, and chop in food processor. Mix in brown sugar, softened cream cheese, Grand Marnier liqueur, and ½ cup ground toasted hazelnuts.

Egg Yolk Glaze

1 egg yolk
1 tablespoon cold water
• Pinch salt

❧

Whisk ingredients together and refrigerate.

Orange Glaze

1 cup sifted confectioner's
    (powdered) sugar
1 teaspoon melted butter
1 teaspoon orange zest
    (see Glossary, pages 123-124)
1 tablespoon Grand Marnier liqueur
• Milk

❧

Mix sugar, butter, orange zest and Grand Marnier together. Add enough milk to make a thin glaze.

NOTE: Most of the flours we use today have been processed enough at the mill that sifting is unnecessary. Unless directed to sift flour in the recipe, it should be measured unsifted. To measure a cup of flour, first stir the flour with a spoon to aerate. Scoop up a heaping cup of flour, and with a knife, sweep the top of the cup to remove the excess. Only if the recipe calls for "sifted flour" should the flour be sifted before measuring.

DID YOU KNOW… That unlike other fruiting trees, the hazelnut tree blooms and pollinates in the middle of winter. Wind carries the pollen from yellow catkins to a tiny red flower, where it stays dormant until June, when the nut begins to form.

Sweet Rolls

This is a good basic sweet roll dough, a little on the sticky side, but still easy to work with. I like to make half of the dough into Cinnamon Rolls and half into Hazelnut Caramel Cups. Both freeze well. The Caramel Cups should be reheated, uncovered, in the oven.

Basic Sweet Roll Dough
2 tablespoons or 2 packages
   (¼ ounce each) active dry yeast
½ cup warm water, 105 to 115 degrees
⅓ cup granulated sugar
½ cup (1 stick) softened butter
2 large eggs
¾ cup warm milk, 105 to 115 degrees
1 teaspoon salt
5 cups unbleached white flour

Stir yeast, warm water, and two table-spoons of the sugar together in large mixing bowl. Let stand until foamy, about three minutes.

Mix in remaining sugar, butter, eggs, milk and salt. Add two cups of the flour and beat with an electric mixer, until the consistency of thick cake batter, about two minutes. Gradually mix in remaining flour. With heavy duty mixer, or by hand, knead until dough is smooth and elastic.

Place in greased bowl, turn to coat the entire ball, cover with dampened kitchen towel, and let rise in warm place until doubled in bulk, about 1½ hours.

Turn out onto lightly floured surface, punch down to release all of the air bubbles and form into desired shapes.

Cinnamon Rolls

½ recipe Basic Sweet Roll dough
2 tablespoons melted butter
⅓ cup brown sugar
1 teaspoon ground cinnamon
½ cup coarsely chopped hazelnuts
½ cup raisins, optional

On lightly floured surface, roll dough out into a 14 x 10 inch rectangle. Brush with melted butter. Sprinkle with the remaining ingredients. Starting from the long side, roll the dough into a log. Pinch the seam together with finger tips. Cut into 12 pieces and place on a greased baking sheet. Flatten slightly with the palm of your hand and press in any ingredients that may have fallen out.

Cover with lightly oiled plastic wrap and let rise until a slight indentation remains when lightly touched with fingertips, about 45 minutes. Shortly before baking, position a baking rack in the center of the oven and heat oven to 375 degrees. Bake on the center rack of a 375-degree oven until lightly browned, about 18 to 20 minutes. Remove from the oven and cool on racks. Spread with Confectioner's Sugar Glaze (page 88) if desired.

Hazelnut Caramel Cups

½ recipe Basic Sweet Roll dough
½ cup, plus 2 tablespoons, melted butter
    (1 stick plus 2 tablespoons)
1 cup brown sugar
1 cup coarsely chopped toasted hazelnuts

Prepare two standard 12-cup nonstick muffin tins by placing one teaspoon each of the brown sugar, melted butter, and hazelnuts—in that order—in each of the cups. Set aside.

On a lightly floured surface, roll dough out into a 20 x 8 inch rectangle. Brush with two tablespoons of the melted butter. Sprinkle with remaining brown sugar and hazelnuts. Starting from the long end, roll the dough into a log. Pinch the seam together with fingertips. Cut into 24 slices and place in prepared muffin tins.

Cover with lightly oiled plastic wrap and let rise until a slight indentation remains when lightly pressed with fingertips, about 45 minutes. Shortly before baking, position a baking rack in the center of the oven and heat oven to 375 degrees. Bake on the center rack of a 375-degree oven until lightly browned, about 18 to 20 minutes. Remove from oven and place a cooling rack on top of the pan. Flip over so that the pan is on the top and let stand for about one minute. Slowly remove the pan. If any of the caramel sticks to the pan, scrape it out with a knife and spread on top of rolls.

Cool on racks.

NOTE: Some people question whether it is necessary to proof rapid rising (instant) dry yeast. Some recipes direct that yeast be added, dry, to the flour. I prefer proofing the yeast, as this is a good indicator that it is fresh and alive. It also insures that all of the yeast is dissolved. Yeast is a living organism and can be destroyed if it gets too hot. Newer yeasts have higher temperature tolerances, but if yeast is exposed to temperatures over about 130 degrees, it becomes ineffective. Dry yeast left in a closed car in the summer may not survive. However, it doesn't mind the cold. Yeast should be stored in the refrigerator or freezer.

Sour Cream Nut Twists

EASE OF
PREPARATION: 3

PREPARATION TIME:
30 TO 45 MINUTES

RISING TIME:
1½ TO 2 HOURS

BAKING TIME:
18 TO 20 MINUTES

YIELD:
36 TWISTS

DID YOU KNOW...
That hazelnuts
mature during the
summer months,
turning from green
to shades of hazel,
and are harvested in
the fall when the
nuts fall to the
ground. They are
then swept into
windrows and
picked up by a
harvester.

These tender sweet rolls earn raves for breakfast or brunch. They freeze well and can be reheated in the oven or microwave. Try both fillings, or if your prefer just one, double the filling recipe to make enough for the entire recipe.

Dough
1 tablespoon or 1 (¼ ounce) package
    active dry yeast
½ cup warm water (105 to 115 degrees)
½ cup granulated sugar, divided
½ cup (1 stick) softened butter
½ cup sour cream
3 large eggs
1 teaspoon salt
5 cups unbleached white flour

Stir yeast, warm water, and two tablespoons of the sugar together in large mixing bowl. Let stand until foamy, about three minutes. Mix in remaining sugar, butter, sour cream, eggs, and salt. Add two cups of the flour and beat with electric mixer until the consistency of thick cake batter, about two minutes. Gradually mix in remaining flour. With heavy duty mixer, or by hand, knead until dough is smooth and elastic.

Place in greased bowl, turn to coat the entire ball, cover with dampened kitchen towel, and let rise in warm place (about 75 to 80 degrees) away from drafts, until doubled in bulk, about one hour.

Turn out onto lightly floured surface, punch down to release all the air bubbles, cut dough in half and form one piece into an 18-inch-long by 12-inch-wide rectangle. Spread half of the rectangle with one of the fillings, spreading to within ½ inch of the edges. Lightly brush edges with cold water.

Fold the other half over the filling, lightly pressing edges together to seal. Cut into one inch strips. Give each piece a double twist and place on lightly greased baking sheet, about one inch apart. Cover with oiled plastic wrap and let rise until almost doubled, about 30 to 45 minutes. Repeat with the remaining dough, using the other filling.

Shortly before baking, position a baking rack in the center of the oven and heat oven to 375 degrees. Bake on the center rack of a 375-degree oven until golden, about 18 to 20 minutes. Remove from the oven and cool on racks. Drizzle with Confectioner's Sugar Glaze. Sprinkle with additional hazelnuts if desired.

Cream Cheese Nut Filling
¼ cup brown sugar
2 tablespoons cream cheese, softened
1 tablespoon hazelnut liqueur
    (such as Frangelico)
½ cup ground toasted hazelnuts

In small bowl mix ingredients together.

Apricot Nut Filling
½ cup ground toasted hazelnuts
⅓ cup apricot jelly
2 teaspoons orange zest
    (See Glossary, pages 123-124)

In small bowl mix ingredients together.

Confectioner's Sugar Glaze
2 cups sifted confectioner's
    (powdered) sugar
3 tablespoons milk
1 tablespoon melted butter

Mix all ingredients together until smooth, adding additional confectioner's sugar or milk to make a thick glaze.

Quick breads are just that—quick to fix, quick to bake, and quickly gone from the table. And too, the baker needs to be quick about getting them into the oven because of the fast-acting leavening agent, baking powder.

Most of the baking powder that is on the shelves today is double acting. First it is activated when the liquid comes in contact with the powder. This is easy to see. When the moist ingredients are first mixed with the dry, and are allowed to set for a few minutes, the batter starts to get puffy. For this reason it is necessary to have all the ingredients assembled and the oven heated before starting to make quick breads. When the batter is put in a hot oven, the heat activates it again and the batter is on the rise.

There are several ways to mix the dry ingredients together so that the leavening is evenly distributed throughout the batter. The most common method directs that the dry ingredients be sifted together. However, there are other methods that work as well, or even better. Whisking the ingredients together is one method. Mixing in a dry work bowl in the food processor is another. To compare these methods, place a teaspoon of cinnamon in two cups of flour and see how well each method works.

Although most often in this book you are directed to whisk the dry ingredients, you may use any of these methods.

Most of these quick breads are pretty easy and foolproof, but it is important not to overmix them. Of course, get them in the oven quickly! No need to run a marathon, but don't let them sit around too long!

Cherry Cream Cheese Coffee Cake

If you love cheesecake, you now can have it for breakfast, too. The crunchy hazelnuts add a nice contrast to the smooth, creamy filling.

This recipe comes from my cooking class assistant, recipe tester and friend, Mary Ann Stadeli. One of the Northwest's great cooks, Mary Ann not only cooks for her family, she also finds time to run a nursery, collect antiques and always lend a hand where needed.

Cream Cheese Filling

8 ounces cream cheese, softened
⅓ cup granulated sugar
2 large eggs
1 tablespoon fresh lemon juice
1 teaspoon lemon zest
　　(See Glossary, pages 123-124)

In food processor, or with electric mixer, beat cream cheese, sugar, eggs, and lemon juice, and lemon zest. Transfer to small bowl and set aside.

Coffee Cake

2¼ cups all purpose flour
¾ cup granulated sugar
2 teaspoons baking powder
½ teaspoon baking soda
¼ teaspoon salt
¾ cup cold butter, cut in ½-inch pieces
½ cup finely chopped, toasted hazelnuts
¾ cup sour cream
1 egg, slightly beaten
1 cup prepared cherry pie filling
½ cup coarsely chopped, toasted hazelnuts

Position a baking rack in the bottom third of the oven and heat oven to 350 degrees. Grease a nine-inch spring-form pan with solid shortening.

Place flour, sugar, baking powder, baking soda, and salt in a food processor bowl fitted with a metal blade. Pulse several times to blend. Add butter and nuts and process until mixture is crumbly, about 20 seconds. Remove one cup of the mixture and reserve.

Add sour cream and egg and process just until evenly moistened. Do not over-process.

Spread batter evenly over the bottom and two inches up the sides of the prepared pan, taking care that the batter is not too thick around the edges. Pour reserved cream cheese filling over batter. Spoon cherry filling over cream cheese and sprinkle with reserved crumbs and coarsely chopped hazelnuts.

Bake in the bottom third of a 350-degree oven for 60 minutes or until the center is set. Let stand for about 15 minutes and loosen the ring from the pan. Cool to room temperature before removing the bottom of the pan.

NOTE: Sour cream can vary a great deal in thickness, so if the batter is very thick, several tablespoons of milk may be added to make it easier to handle. The batter should be about like soft biscuit dough.

EASE OF
PREPARATION: 2

PREPARATION TIME:
20 MINUTES

BAKING TIME:
60 MINUTES

SPECIAL
EQUIPMENT:
9 INCH SPRING
FORM PAN

YIELD:
10 TO 12 SERVINGS

PHOTO:
SEE OPPOSITE PAGE

NOTE: Leftovers may be frozen. Reheat very gently in the microwave so that the cream cheese filling does not get too hot.

Lemon, Blueberry, & Hazelnut Tea Bread

EASE OF
PREPARATION: 1

PREPARATION TIME:
10 MINUTES

BAKING TIME:
55 TO 60 MINUTES

YIELD: 1 LOAF
(BAKED LOAF MAY
BE FROZEN)

FOR PHOTO:
SEE PAGE 90

NOTE: If using
frozen blueberries,
make sure they are
thawed. Pat them
dry to remove any
excess moisture.

Just a hint of lemon brings out the toasty flavor of roasted hazelnuts. No need to serve this bread with butter. It is fine just the way it comes out of the oven.

2 cups all purpose white flour
1½ teaspoons baking powder
½ teaspoon salt
¼ teaspoon baking soda
½ cup (1 stick) butter, room temperature
¾ cup sugar
2 teaspoons lemon zest
   (See Glossary, pages 123-124)
2 whole large eggs
½ cup milk
2 tablespoons poppy seeds
1 cup fresh or frozen blueberries, thawed
¾ cup coarsely chopped hazelnuts

Position a baking rack in the lower third of the oven and heat oven to 350 degrees. Generously grease a 8 x 4 x 3 inch loaf pan with solid shortening. Dust lightly with flour; tap out excess.

In a small bowl, whisk together flour, baking powder, salt, and soda.

With an electric mixer, in a large mixing bowl, beat butter, sugar, and lemon zest until well mixed. Add eggs, one at a time, and beat until light and fluffy. Alternately beat in milk and dry ingredients until mixture is smooth. Mix in poppy seeds. Fold in blueberries and ½ cup hazelnuts.

Pour batter into prepared pan, sprinkle with remaining hazelnuts, and bake in the lower third of a 350-degree oven for about 60 minutes, or until the top springs back when lightly touched with fingertips, and a pick inserted into the center comes out clean. Let stand for several minutes, run a knife around the edge of the loaf to loosen and unmold onto cooling rack.

Fresh Pear & Nut Muffins

In addition to pears, other fruits, such as bananas, apples, peaches, blueberries, or mangoes work well in this recipe, too.

1 medium fresh pear
 (can use well-drained canned pear)
1¼ cups all purpose white flour
2 teaspoons baking powder
½ teaspoon baking soda
½ teaspoon salt
⅛ teaspoon freshly grated nutmeg
½ cup oat bran
½ cup finely chopped, toasted hazelnuts
⅔ cup granulated sugar
¼ cup melted butter
1 large egg
½ cup plain yogurt
2 tablespoons fresh lemon juice

Place the baking rack in the upper third of the oven and heat the oven to 400 degrees. Generously grease muffin pans with solid shortening or spray with nonstick vegetable spray.

Peel, core, and dice pear into ¼-inch pieces. Set aside.

In a medium bowl, whisk together flour, baking powder, baking soda, salt, and nutmeg; stir in oat bran and hazelnuts.

In a large bowl, beat sugar, butter, egg, yogurt, and lemon juice until well mixed. Stir in dry ingredients just until flour disappears. Fold in pear.

Fill prepared muffin tins almost to the top. Lightly sprinkle topping on muffins, dividing evenly among the cups. Bake in the upper third of a 400-degree oven for about 12 to 15 minutes for the miniature muffins, or 18 to 20 minutes for the large, or until the center springs back when lightly touched. Let cool for several minutes before removing from pans. Cool on racks.

Crumb Topping

1 tablespoon granulated sugar
1 tablespoon all purpose flour
1 tablespoon finely chopped,
 toasted hazelnuts
2 teaspoons cold butter
⅛ teaspoon freshly grated nutmeg

In a food processor, or with a pastry blender, mix all ingredients together until crumbly.

NOTE: It really pays in the long run to invest in good, nonstick muffin pans. Short of that, be sure to get the cups thoroughly coated with shortening or vegetable spray. I've tried using paper cups, but it seems the muffins just stick to the paper rather than to the pan!

EASE OF
PREPARATION: 1

PREPARATION TIME:
15 MINUTES

BAKING TIME
STANDARD
MUFFINS:
18 TO 20 MINUTES

BAKING TIME
MINIATURE
MUFFINS:
12 TO 15 MINUTES

SPECIAL
EQUIPMENT:
MINIATURE MUFFIN
PANS, OPTIONAL

YIELD:
12 LARGE OR
36 MINIATURE
MUFFINS

FOR PHOTO:
SEE PAGE 90

Cranberry, Orange, & Hazelnut Scones

EASE OF
PREPARATION: 1

PREPARATION TIME:
15 MINUTES

BAKING TIME:
12 TO 15 MINUTES

YIELD: 12 SCONES

DID YOU KNOW . . .
That hazelnuts are
high in fiber and in
a number of
minerals and
vitamins such as
calcium, potassium,
magnesium, and
Vitamins C and E.
They are very low
in sugars and salt.

Although I have nothing but respect for labor-saving devices, especially the food processor, I prefer the texture of scones made by hand—literally. I like to smash the cold chunks of butter into the flour with my fingertips until they are just the right size—some about the size of peas, some a little larger, and some a little smaller. This layering of the chunks of butter is what makes the scones flaky.

2 cups all purpose flour
⅓ cup granulated sugar
2 teaspoons baking powder
½ teaspoon baking soda
½ teaspoon salt
¼ cup (½ stick) cold butter
½ cup dried cranberries
½ cup coarsely chopped,
   toasted hazelnuts
2 teaspoons orange zest
   (See Glossary, pages 123-124)
1 large egg, slightly beaten
⅔ cup buttermilk

Position a baking rack in the upper third of the oven and heat oven to 425 degrees.

In a large bowl, whisk together the flour, sugar, baking powder, baking soda, and salt.

With a pastry blender or with your fingertips, cut butter into dry ingredients until the largest pieces are the size of peas. Mix in cranberries, hazelnuts, and orange zest.

Whisk egg and buttermilk together and pour all at once into dry ingredients. Stir just until the dry ingredients are evenly moistened.

Turn out onto a lightly floured surface and knead four or five times. Divide dough in half and form into two six-inch rounds, about ¾-inch thick in the center. Cut each round into six wedges and place one inch apart on a lightly greased baking sheet.

Bake in the upper third of a 425-degree oven until golden, about 12 to 15 minutes. Cool on rack and serve with Orange Hazelnut Butter.

Orange Hazelnut Butter
½ cup (1 stick) butter, room temperature
¼ cup orange juice
2 tablespoons honey
1 tablespoon orange zest
⅓ cup finely chopped hazelnuts

With electric mixer beat butter until smooth. With the mixer running, slowly drizzle in orange juice and continue beating until fluffy. Mix in honey, orange zest, and hazelnuts. Serve with warm scones.

Uncle Matt Gerspacher was never one to impose on folks. On his rare visits (always for three days or less) he liked to do his part by making pancakes for breakfast.

Unfortunately, his recipe called for "a little of this" and "some of that." I have taken liberties with his formula, but I know that Uncle Matt would definitely approve of the warm Hazelnut Syrup, laced with Frangelico.

Uncle Matt's Famous Buttermilk Pancakes

Buttermilk Pancakes

2 cups all purpose white flour

1 teaspoon baking soda

½ teaspoon salt

3 whole large eggs, separated

2 tablespoons brown sugar

1½ cups buttermilk

3 tablespoons melted butter

• Vegetable oil for frying

In a small bowl, whisk together flour, soda, and salt. In a separate bowl, whip egg whites until they hold firm, moist peaks.

In a large bowl, beat egg yolks and brown sugar until blended. Mix in buttermilk, melted butter, and dry ingredients, beating just until evenly moistened. Do not over-mix. Gently fold in egg whites.

In the meantime, heat a nonstick griddle to about 350 degrees. Very lightly, brush with vegetable oil. Ladle the batter onto the hot griddle, about ⅓ cup per pancake, smoothing out with the back of the ladle. Cook until the pancakes are puffy, bubbles form and break, and the tops are dull. Turn and cook the other side. Brush the griddle with oil between each batch if they start to stick. Serve with hot syrup.

Hazelnut Syrup with Frangelico

2 tablespoons butter

⅓ cup medium chopped toasted hazelnuts

2 tablespoons Frangelico
    (hazelnut liqueur)

½ cup maple syrup

Melt butter in small saucepan. Add hazelnuts and toss to coat with butter. Add Frangelico and syrup and simmer for several minutes. Serve warm.

EASE OF
PREPARATION: 1

PREPARATION TIME:
15 MINUTES

COOKING TIME:
10 TO 15 MINUTES TO
COOK THE BATCH

YIELD: 12 TO 16
LARGE PANCAKES

NOTE: The batter
will thicken when
standing. Add a little
more buttermilk if
necessary.

Mile-High Hazelnut Popovers

EASE OF
PREPARATION: 1

PREPARATION TIME:
10 MINUTES

BAKING TIME:
25 TO 35 MINUTES IN
BRUSHED STEEL OR
CAST IRON POPOVER
PANS—35 TO 45
MINUTES IN
ALUMINUM MUFFIN
PANS

YIELD:
8 POPOVERS

NOTE: The type of
pan used for this
recipe will make a
big difference in the
baking time. The
recipe works best
when baked in
traditional heavy
cast iron or brushed
steel popover pans
that are narrow at
the bottom and wide
at the top. They may
be baked in an
aluminum muffin tin,
although they will
not pop quite as
high, and the baking
time, at 375 degrees,
will need to be
increased as
directed.

This recipe lives up to its name. The crusty, nut-flavored puffs seem to reach astronomical heights when the recipe is followed exactly. Carmen Jones, Certified Culinary Professional Chef/Instructor of baking and fine cuisine for 25 years, developed this recipe and generously shares it with us.

¼ cup chopped toasted hazelnuts
3 large eggs (use extra-large if available)
1 cup milk
3 tablespoons heavy cream
1 teaspoon salt
1 cup sifted all purpose white flour
¼ cup vegetable oil

Place hazelnuts in a blender or food processor and chop until fine. Add eggs, milk, cream, and salt to the blender or food processor and process on high speed until very smooth. Add flour and mix or blend again on high speed until very smooth. Cover and chill the batter for at least two hours.

Position an oven rack in the top third of the oven, put popover pan in cold oven and preheat all to 450 degrees. Open the oven and, using a pastry brush, generously oil eight popover cups. Close oven for about two minutes. Re-open and pour the well-mixed batter into heated/oiled pans, almost to the brim. Carefully close the oven and bake for ten minutes. Reduce temperature to 375 degrees and bake for another 15 to 25 minutes if using brushed steel or cast iron popover pans. Bake for another 25 to 40 minutes if using aluminum muffin tins, or until golden brown and puffed high.

Loosen popovers with a knife, remove from the hot pan, and serve immediately with sweet butter.

NOTE: This recipe may be doubled. If refrigerated, batter can be held for up to eight hours.

Say "cookies and milk," and a different image pops into each person's mind, but you can always count on a smile on the face. Whether it is a childhood memory of coming home from school greeted by the wafting perfume of freshly baked cookies, or of the delight of your own children dashing in for a sweet surprise, cookies are the ultimate in comfort food.

The following recipes showcase hazelnuts, of course, but almost any cookie will only get better with the addition of toasted hazelnuts. Try ground hazelnuts in Russian Tea Cakes, Thumbprints, or sugar cookies. Chunks of hazelnuts shine in brownies, fruit cookies, and even peanut butter cookies. Tiny helpful hands can expertly sprinkle chopped nuts on cut out cookies and gingerbread roofs.

Cookies should always be baked in a pre-heated oven. A sturdy aluminum cookie sheet with a narrow rim will bake the most evenly. A cushion type pan with airspace between two thin metal sheets will prevent burning if you have a very small oven where the heat cannot properly circulate around the pan. For even browning when baking two sheets of cookies at once, be sure to rotate the pans about halfway through the baking time.

Although the baking times and temperatures in the recipes are as accurate as possible, factors may vary in your own kitchen. The temperature of the ingredients, the type of pan used, and the calibration of the oven are all factors that can affect baking times. Therefore, it is a good idea to check on the cookies about two minutes before the end of the minimum baking time. The nose is also a good indicator of doneness. When you can smell the cookies, check them out!

Double Nut Chocolate Chip Cookies

The quest is on for the ultimate chocolate chip cookie. This one just might be it. It is a little soft, a little chewy, just a good "cookies and milk" chocolate chip cookie.

2 cups all purpose white flour
½ teaspoon baking powder
½ teaspoon salt
¼ teaspoon baking soda
½ cup finely ground toasted hazelnuts
⅔ cup brown sugar
½ cup granulated sugar
½ cup unsalted butter, room temperature
½ cup solid shortening
1 large egg
¼ cup sour cream
2 teaspoons hazelnut liqueur,
   (such as Frangelico)
1 cup chocolate chips
½ cup coarsely chopped toasted hazelnuts

Position a baking rack in the center of the oven and heat oven to 375 degrees.

In a small bowl, thoroughly whisk together flour, baking powder, salt, and baking soda. Whisk in finely ground nuts.

With an electric mixer, beat brown sugar, granulated sugar, butter, and shortening in a large bowl until smooth. Add egg, sour cream, and hazelnut liqueur and beat until smooth and light. Beat in dry ingredients.

With a rubber spatula, mix in chocolate chips and coarsely chopped hazelnuts.

For monster cookies, drop two ounces of dough in a mound, about five inches apart, on a lightly greased cookie sheet. Bake in the center of a 375-degree oven for about 12 to 15 minutes or until light golden color. Let sit in pan for several minutes, remove with spatula and cool on racks.

For "normal" sized cookies, drop about one ounce (a generous tablespoon) of dough on a lightly greased cookie sheet, and bake in a 375-degree oven for about 12 minutes.

NOTE: Two teaspoons vanilla extract may be used in place of the hazelnut liqueur.

EASE OF
PREPARATION: 2

PREPARATION TIME:
15 MINUTES

BAKING TIME:
12 TO 15 MINUTES

YIELD: 16 - 4 INCH
COOKIES OR
32 - 2 INCH COOKIES

FOR PHOTO:
SEE OPPOSITE PAGE

DID YOU KNOW . . .
That Oregon hazelnuts are prized for their characteristically large kernels.

Orange Hazelnut Oatmeal Cookies

EASE OF
PREPARATION: 2

CHILLING TIME:
1 HOUR

PREPARATION TIME:
15 MINUTES

BAKING TIME:
12 TO 14 MINUTES

YIELD: 48 - 2 1/2 INCH
COOKIES

Sharon Bamford, who lives in the heart of hazelnut country, has made this recipe for her family for a number of years. She doubles the recipe and still they disappear faster than she can make them!

1½ cups all purpose white flour
½ teaspoon baking soda
½ teaspoon salt
½ cup butter, room temperature
½ cup solid shortening
¾ cup granulated sugar
¾ cup brown sugar, packed
2 large eggs
2 teaspoons vanilla
2 tablespoons orange zest
    (See Glossary, pages 123-124)
¼ cup orange juice
2½ cups oatmeal
1 cup coarsely chopped toasted hazelnuts

Position a baking rack in the center of the oven and heat oven to 375 degrees.

In a bowl, whisk together flour, baking soda, and salt.

In a large bowl, beat butter, shortening, and sugars together until smooth, about two minutes. Add eggs and vanilla and continue beating until light and fluffy, about two more minutes. Mix in orange zest. Add dry ingredients and orange juice alternately in three additions. Fold in oatmeal and hazelnuts. Chill the dough for about one hour.

Drop 1½ tablespoons of dough, two inches apart on a lightly greased cookie sheet. Flatten slightly with the palm of the hand and bake in the center of a 375-degree oven until golden, about 12 minutes. Let cool in the pan for several minutes; remove with metal spatula and cool on racks.

Crispy, buttery shortbread is always a favorite. The chocolate edge adds a touch of elegance. These cookies are especially good with a cup of herbal tea.

1 cup all-purpose flour
½ teaspoon baking powder
¼ teaspoon salt
½ cup butter, room temperature
⅓ cup brown sugar
½ cup finely chopped toasted hazelnuts
½ cup semi-sweet chocolate pieces

Position a baking rack in the center of the oven and heat oven to 325 degrees.

In a small bowl, whisk together flour, baking powder, and salt. Set aside.

In a medium bowl, with electric mixer, beat butter and sugar together for about two minutes, or until the mixture is smooth and creamy. Mix in dry ingredients and ground nuts.

Form the mixture into a ball and place between two large pieces of plastic wrap. With fingertips, gently smooth out into a round slightly larger than eight inches in diameter. Try to keep the dough thickness as even as possible, about ¼ inch thick.

Hazelnut Shortbread Dipped in Chocolate

Refrigerate until firm, about 20 minutes.

Remove plastic wrap and place dough on cookie sheet. Using an eight-inch plate as a guide, trim off uneven edges, leaving a smooth eight-inch round. With a pizza cutter or knife, cut dough into 12 wedges.

Bake in the center of a 325-degree oven for about 20 minutes, or until the dough is set and the edges are just slightly golden. Remove from oven and immediately re-score the dough. Let cool on baking sheet.

In a microwave or the top half of a double boiler, melt chocolate to about 85 degrees. Dip the rounded edge of the shortbread about one inch into the chocolate. Gently shake off excess and place on waxed paper to dry.

EASE OF PREPARATION: 2

PREPARATION TIME: 10 MINUTES

CHILLING TIME: 20 MINUTES

BAKING TIME: 20 MINUTES

YIELD: 12 COOKIES

Just see if they can guess the secret ingredient in these cookies.

1¾ cups all purpose white flour
½ teaspoon baking soda
¼ teaspoon salt
½ cup finely chopped toasted hazelnuts
⅔ cup granulated sugar
½ cup butter, room temperature (1 stick)
1 large egg
1 tablespoon fresh lemon juice
1 tablespoon chopped fresh lemon thyme
2 teaspoons lemon zest
    (See Glossary, pages 123-124)

In a small bowl, whisk together flour, baking soda, and salt. Stir in hazelnuts. In a large bowl, beat sugar and butter with electric mixer until light and creamy. Beat in egg, lemon juice, thyme, and lemon zest. Mix in dry ingredients.

Hazelnut Thyme & Lemon Cookies

Transfer dough to a large piece of plastic wrap and form into a 12-inch-long log. Refrigerate for several hours, or freeze for 30 minutes, until firm. (Dough may be kept in the refrigerator for several days or in the freezer for up to one month.)

Shortly before baking, position a baking rack in center of oven and heat to 350 degrees. Slice dough into ¼-inch-thick slices and place about one inch apart on lightly greased baking sheet. Bake in center of a 350-degree oven for about ten minutes, or just slightly brown. Cool on racks.

EASE OF PREPARATION: 1

PREPARATION TIME: 15 MINUTES

BAKING TIME: 10 MINUTES

YIELD: ABOUT 4 DOZEN

101

Lemon Raspberry & Hazelnut Bars

EASE OF
PREPARATION: 2

SPECIAL
EQUIPMENT:
11 X 7 GLASS BAKING
DISH

PREPARATION TIME:
20 MINUTES

BAKING TIME:
40 MINUTES

YIELD: 35 BARS

DID YOU KNOW . . .
That Europeans
consume about 2.1
pounds of hazelnuts
per capita per year.

*This is a new twist on an old favorite.
However, eat them while they are fresh, as they
don't freeze well.*

Dough
1½ cups all purpose white flour
⅔ cup sifted confectioners
    (powdered) sugar
½ teaspoon salt
¾ cup (1½ sticks) cold unsalted butter,
    cut in ½ inch pieces
½ cup finely chopped, toasted hazelnuts

Lemon Raspberry Topping
¾ cup granulated sugar
3 3-inch-long strips lemon peel,
    cut in ½ inch pieces
3 large eggs
¼ cup fresh lemon juice
¼ cup all purpose white flour
½ cup raspberry jam
½ cup coarsely chopped, toasted hazelnuts

Position a baking rack in the center of
the oven and heat oven to 350 degrees.

Spray a 7 x 11 inch baking dish with
nonstick vegetable spray.

Place flour, confectioners sugar, and salt
in the bowl of a food processor fitted with a
metal blade. Pulse several times until well
mixed. Add butter and process for about
30 seconds, or until the mixture is like
coarse meal. Add nuts and pulse two or
three times. The mixture will be very
crumbly. Remove one cup of the dough
and reserve.

Pour remaining dough into prepared
baking pan. With fingertips, press the
dough evenly into pan. Bake in the center
of a 350-degree oven until just set, about
18 minutes.

In the meantime, prepare the Lemon
Raspberry Topping. Place sugar and lemon
peel into a work bowl of a food processor
fitted with a metal blade and process for
one to two minutes or until lemon is very
fine. Add eggs, lemon juice, and flour.
Process until smooth, about 30 seconds.

After dough is set, remove from oven
and gently spread raspberry jam evenly
over the top to within one-half inch of the
edges. Pour reserved lemon topping over
jam and return to oven for another 15
minutes, or until lemon is just barely set.

Again, remove from oven and sprinkle
reserved dough and coarsely chopped
hazelnuts over the top. Return to oven just
until topping just starts to turn golden,
about eight minutes.

When cool, cut into one by two inch
strips.

Coconut Hazelnut Refrigerator Cookies

With this recipe the kids can have fresh baked cookies every day. Just slice and bake as many as you want, and refrigerate the remaining dough. Both the dough and the baked cookies freeze well.

2 cups all purpose white flour
½ teaspoon baking soda
¼ teaspoon salt
½ cup brown sugar
½ cup granulated sugar
6 tablespoons unsalted butter,
    room temperature
1 large egg
½ teaspoon coconut extract, optional
¼ cup heavy (whipping) cream
¾ cup flaked coconut
1½ cups finely chopped, toasted hazelnuts,
    divided

In a small bowl, whisk flour, baking soda, and salt together. Set aside.

In a large bowl, with an electric mixer, beat sugars and butter until smooth and creamy, about two minutes. Beat in egg and coconut extract.

Alternately mix in dry ingredients and cream, in several additions. Stir in coconut and ½ cup finely chopped hazelnuts.

Turn dough out onto an 18-inch-long sheet of plastic wrap and form into a log about 12 inches long and two inches in diameter. Roll the log in the remaining hazelnuts, pressing firmly into the dough.

Wrap the log tightly in the plastic wrap and refrigerate for at least two hours, or freeze for 30 minutes.

TO BAKE: Position a baking rack in the center of the oven and heat oven to 350 degrees. Slice dough into ¼-inch slices and place on an ungreased cooking sheet. Bake in the center of the a 350-degree oven for about ten minutes, or until cookies are just set and start to turn golden. Cool on racks.

EASE OF
PREPARATION: 1

PREPARATION TIME:
15 MINUTES

BAKING TIME:
10 MINUTES

CHILLING TIME:
2 HOURS, PLUS

YIELD:
4 DOZEN COOKIES

Nutty Cream Cheese Brownies

5/21/01

EASE OF
PREPARATION: 2

PREPARATION TIME:
15 MINUTES

BAKING TIME:
35 TO 40 MINUTES

YIELD:
4 DOZEN COOKIES

These extra fudgy brownies will suit just about any taste. Because everyone wants a center piece with the most filling, there is a very generous amount of cream cheese filling.

4 ounces unsweetened chocolate
1 cup granulated sugar
½ cup unsalted butter, room temperature
1 teaspoon vanilla
3 large eggs
⅔ cup all purpose flour
½ teaspoon baking powder
½ teaspoon salt
¾ cup coarsely chopped toasted hazelnuts

Position baking rack in center of oven and heat to 350 degrees. Generously butter a 7 x 11 inch glass baking dish.

In the top half of a double boiler, or in microwave, melt chocolate. Cool slightly.

In a small bowl, whisk together flour, baking powder, and salt.

In a mixing bowl, beat sugar and butter together with an electric mixer until smooth, about two minutes. Add vanilla and eggs, one at a time, beating well after each addition. Mix in chocolate and dry ingredients just until flour disappears. Fold in hazelnuts.

Pour half of the batter into the prepared pan. Top with cream cheese mixture and spread with the remaining chocolate batter.

Bake in the center of a 350-degree oven for 35 minutes, or until the center is set. Do not overbake. Cool in pan and frost with Chocolate Frosting.

Cream Cheese Filling

8 ounces cream cheese, room temperature
2 tablespoon unsalted butter,
    room temperature
⅓ cup granulated sugar
1 tablespoon cornstarch
1 large egg
2 tablespoons milk
1 teaspoon vanilla

In a mixing bowl, beat cream cheese, butter, and sugar with an electric mixer until smooth. Add remaining ingredients and beat until well blended.

Chocolate Frosting

6 ounces semisweet chocolate, chopped
¼ cup unsalted butter
¼ cup whipping cream
1 teaspoon vanilla
1 cup sifted confectioner's sugar

In the top half of a double boiler or in the microwave, melt chocolate and butter together. Stir in cream and vanilla. Beat in confectioner's sugar and cool until it is of spreading consistency.

Selecting the perfect chocolate is almost an art form, requiring practice and experience and—best of all—lots of sampling. Because cocoa butter melts at mouth temperature, a piece of good quality chocolate, high in cocoa butter, almost effortlessly melts in the mouth. If it needs to be chewed, it very likely contains paraffin-like additives which melt at higher temperatures. Sometimes terminology used for different types of chocolate can be confusing. Often both couverture chocolate and confectioner's coatings (compound chocolates) are referred to as dipping chocolate. However, couverture chocolate is a very high grade used by chocolatiers to produce that thin, glossy coating that distinguishes fine chocolates and truffles. When used for dipping and molding, it must be tempered in order to harden well and avoid becoming soft, dull, and streaked. Confectioners' coatings often have additional ingredients that affect texture and flavor, but it unmolds easily and works very well for chocolate art and decorations. Best of all, it does not need tempering.

Dark chocolate—bittersweet, semisweet, or unsweetened—is the easiest form with which to work. Milk chocolate and white chocolate both contain milk solids, and some brands can be a little more difficult to melt smoothly. Although tempering is not difficult, it does take a certain amount of patience and a good, accurate thermometer. (NOTE: An accurate instant-read thermometer is invaluable for tempering chocolate.) Dark chocolate should be heated to 120 degrees, the temperature at which cocoa butter crystals melt, then cooled to 80 degrees so they are evenly distributed. Do not heat above 120 degrees, or chocolate may tighten, get grainy, or even burn. After chocolate is cooled to 80 degrees, gently reheat to 86 to 90 degrees, so the chocolate is thinner and better for dipping. Above 93 degrees and below 78 degrees the crystals again become unstable and the process must be repeated, so it is important to maintain this temperature range.

Before beginning, plan on working with at least one pound of chocolate; two is better. The chocolate should be grated, shaved, or thinly chopped. Place about ¼ of the chocolate in the top half of a double boiler with the water underneath kept at a temperature of 120 degrees. Do not let water touch the bottom of the pan. Let the chocolate stand until it is melted and gradually stir in remaining chocolate until it is all 120 degrees. Remove from heat and slowly cool to 80 degrees. By the same process reheat the chocolate to 88 degrees for dipping. Now the trick is keeping the temperature at 88 to 90 degrees while dipping. Heating pads, hot water bottles, and heat lamps have all been enlisted for this purpose, but if just dipping a small amount, taking the top of the double boiler on and off the heat should suffice.

Probably the most important rule in working with chocolate is to never allow steam or water to come in contact with the chocolate.

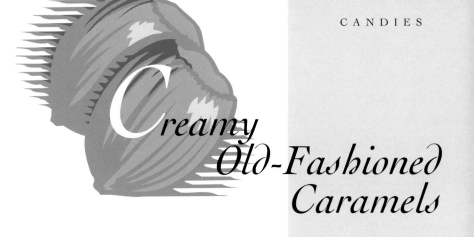

Creamy Old-Fashioned Caramels

This recipe makes just about the best caramels I have ever tasted. It comes from Bonnie Stewart Mickelson's charming cookbook, Hollyhocks & Radishes, *which is a wonderfully readable collection of nostalgic, yet contemporary, recipes.*

Where she lives, in Bellevue, Washington, Bonnie's caramels are somewhat of a legend. They attract high bidders when she donates them to local charity auctions. Although it is hard to improve on perfection, adding hazelnuts and chocolate certainly can't hurt.

2 cups granulated sugar
1 cup (8 ounces) light Karo syrup
3 cups (1½ pints) heavy cream
1 tablespoon butter
• Pinch salt
1 cup coarsely chopped toasted hazelnuts
4 ounces milk chocolate
   (dipping chocolate), melted

Butter a 9 x 13 inch glass baking dish. Hook a candy thermometer on the edge of a heavy Dutch oven or kettle, then place the sugar, syrup, and one cup of the cream in the pot. Bring to a boil over high heat, stirring constantly with a truncated wooden spoon . . . one with a hole in its center is the best.

When the thermometer reaches 236 degrees, add another cup of cream, never ceasing to stir diligently. Add the last cup of cream when the temperature again reaches 236 degrees.

Continue cooking and stirring until it reaches 242 degrees. Immediately remove from the burner and stir in butter, salt, and hazelnuts. When blended in, pour caramel into prepared pan. Cool on a rack.

When completely cooled, run a spatula around the edge of the pan, then invert onto a cutting board or marble slab. Spread melted chocolate evenly over the surface. Let stand until chocolate is set, and then cut into bite-size pieces. Wrap in small pieces of wax paper, twisting the ends to seal.

Tied in plastic bags, the caramels will keep nicely for at least two weeks.

EASE OF
PREPARATION: 2

PREPARATION TIME:
45 MINUTES, EXCEPT
CUTTING TIME

YIELD: 100 PIECES

NOTE: Due to lack of will power, I have cut Bonnie's original recipe in half. The above may be successfully doubled to make 200 pieces.

Dark Chocolate Grand Marnier Truffles

◉ ◉ ◉ ◉

EASE OF
PREPARATION: FROM
1 IF ROLLED IN NUTS
TO 4+ IF DIPPED

PREPARATION TIME:
20 MINUTES
(ADD ANOTHER
HOUR IF DIPPING)

COOLING TIME:
UP TO 1 HOUR

YIELD: 12 TO 15
1 INCH TRUFFLES

FOR TRUFFLES
PHOTO: SEE PAGE 106

NOTE: The easiest
method I have found
for dipping truffles is
to insert a round
toothpick into the
ball, dip in chocolate
and shake off excess.
Slide a fork under
the truffle, placing
the toothpick
between the tines.
Pull out the
toothpick and push
the truffle off the
fork and on to
waxed paper with
the pick.

Nothing quite says "indulgence" like the perfect chocolate truffle with its shiny crisp chocolate shell and creamy, smooth center.

To get that smooth center, egg yolks need to be incorporated into the filling somehow. For years that was a pretty simple task. No one was too concerned about whisking a raw egg yolk into the warm chocolate. We told ourselves that the chocolate was warm enough to cook the egg — maybe.

And then came the salmonella scare. Raw eggs were no longer welcome at the table, and truffles just weren't quite the same.

Now Shirley Corriber, Atlanta food scientist and educator (and truffle lover extraodinaire) has found a way to add the egg yolks, so that food safety will no longer be a problem. Her method, described below, of whisking the yolks into the cream and heating to 160 degrees works beautifully. Be sure to watch the temperature carefully, however, for if it gets much warmer than 160 degrees, the eggs will scramble.

6 ounces good quality semi-sweet
    chocolate, coarsely chopped or shaved
¼ cup unsalted butter
⅓ cup whipping cream
1 egg yolk
1 tablespoon orange liqueur
    (such as Grand Marnier)
2 teaspoons orange zest
    (see Glossary, pages 123-124)
¼ cup finely chopped toasted hazelnuts

◉

In the top half of a double boiler, heat chocolate and butter together just so the chocolate is warm and starts to melt, but is still holding its shape. Remove from heat; stir until entirely melted.

In a saucepan, boil cream over medium high heat until it is reduced by half. Remove from heat and let cool for several minutes. Whisk in egg yolk and return to low heat. Whisk quickly and constantly until the temperature reaches 160 degrees. The mixture will thicken somewhat like hollandaise. Have a saucepan of ice water nearby and place the bottom of the pan in the ice water to immediately stop cooking.

Let the egg mixture cool to lukewarm and whisk into the chocolate mixture. Stir in remaining ingredients and refrigerate, stirring several times, until the mixture is firm enough to scoop and roll into one-inch balls.

Let stand at room temperature (or refrigerate) until firm, about one hour. Dip in tempered chocolate, or when still slightly soft roll in cocoa powder, nuts, or finely shaved chocolate.

NOTE: Finished truffles should be stored in the refrigerator.

IMPORTANT TIP: If you love truffles, but there just isn't time to dip them, roll the balls while they are still slightly soft in cocoa powder, shaved chocolate, flaked coconut or finely chopped toasted hazelnuts.

The lightness of these truffles comes from whipping the ingredients before rolling into balls.

Light Chocolate Ganache Truffles

6 ounces milk chocolate,
     coarsely chopped or shaved
2 tablespoons unsalted butter
⅓ cup whipping cream
1 egg yolk
1 tablespoon hazelnut liqueur
     (such as Frangelico)
¼ cup finely chopped toasted hazelnuts

In the top half of a double boiler, heat chocolate and butter together so the chocolate is warm and starts to melt, but still holds its shape. Remove from heat; stir until melted.

In saucepan, boil cream over medium high heat until it is reduced by half. Remove from heat; let cool several minutes. Whisk in egg yolk and return to low heat.

Whisk quickly and constantly until temperature reaches 160 degrees. The mixture will thicken somewhat like hollandaise. Have a saucepan of ice water nearby and place the bottom of the pan in the ice water if it gets too hot.

Let egg mixture cool to lukewarm and whisk into chocolate mixture. Stir in hazelnut liqueur. Let stand or refrigerate until it reaches room temperature.

With electric mixer, beat mixture just until it is fluffy and light in color. Do not overbeat or it will get grainy. Mix in nuts. Let stand until firm enough to scoop up into balls. Dip in tempered chocolate, or when still slightly soft roll in cocoa powder, nuts, or finely shaved chocolate.

EASE OF
PREPARATION:
VARIES FROM 1 IF
ROLLED IN NUTS TO
4+ IF DIPPED

PREPARATION TIME:
45 MINUTES
(ADD ANOTHER
HOUR IF DIPPING)

CHILLING TIME:
1 HOUR

YIELD: 12 TO 15
1 INCH TRUFFLES

Not everyone may like chocolate. In that case, these white chocolate, coconut, and hazelnut truffles may still satisfy that sweet tooth.

White Chocolate Coconut Truffles

5 ounces good quality white chocolate,
     coarsely chopped or shaved
2 tablespoons unsalted butter
⅓ cup whipping cream
1 egg yolk
¼ cup finely chopped coconut
¼ cup finely chopped toasted hazelnuts
½ teaspoon coconut extract, optional

In the top half of a double boiler, heat chocolate and butter together just so the chocolate is warm and starts to melt, but is still holding its shape. Remove from heat, stir until entirely melted.

In a saucepan, boil the cream over medium high heat until it is reduced by half. Remove from the heat and let cool several minutes. Whisk in egg yolk and return to low heat.

Whisk quickly and constantly until the temperature reaches 160 degrees. The mixture will thicken somewhat like hollandaise. Have a saucepan of ice water nearby and place the bottom of the pan in ice water to immediately stop the cooking.

Let egg mixture cool to lukewarm and whisk into white chocolate mixture. Stir in remaining ingredients and refrigerate, stirring several times, until mixture is firm enough to scoop and roll into one-inch balls. Let stand at room temperature (or refrigerate) until firm, about one hour. Dip in tempered chocolate, or when still slightly soft roll in coconut or nuts.

EASE OF
PREPARATION: FROM
1 IF ROLLED IN NUTS
TO 4+ IF DIPPED

PREPARATION TIME:
20 MINUTES
(ADD ANOTHER
HOUR IF DIPPING)

CHILLING TIME:
1 HOUR

YIELD: 10 TO 12
1-INCH TRUFFLES

109

Hazelnut Brittle

The addition of peanut butter makes this softer than most brittles, but it still has that crunch. If available, use hazelnut butter in place of peanut butter.

1½ cups granulated sugar
½ cup brown sugar
1 cup light corn syrup
¼ cup, plus 2 teaspoons, water
2 cups whole or halved toasted hazelnuts
1 cup creamy style peanut butter
1 teaspoon baking soda

Generously butter a large baking sheet or marble slab.

In a three-quart kettle or saucepan, combine granulated sugar, brown sugar, syrup, and ¼ cup water. Stir until sugar is dissolved. Hook a candy thermometer on the edge of the pan and cook syrup over medium high heat until temperature reaches 280 degrees, about ten minutes.

Add hazelnuts and continue cooking until the mixture turns light brown and reaches 300 degrees, about five minutes.

While the syrup is cooking, heat peanut butter in the top of a double boiler or in a microwave.

Dissolve soda in two teaspoons water. When syrup reaches 300 degrees, remove from heat and quickly stir in peanut butter, and then soda mixture. Immediately pour out onto a buttered surface, pouring as thin as possible. Tip the sheet or slab so that the candy will flow in a thin sheet; however, do not spread it with a knife, or it will loose its light and airy texture.

Let cool and break into serving sized pieces. Store in an airtight container for as long as several weeks.

Americans like to have their cake and eat it too. Trend watchers are constantly perplexed by polls that show both low fat foods and desserts in top place with consumers. We may read the labels and watch the fat, but we still like our indulgences.

"Anything Chocolate" consistently ranks number one when Americans are asked to list their favorite desserts. Because chocolate and hazelnuts have such affinity for one another—and I for them—chocolate desserts definitely dominate the dessert category. But this doesn't mean the other desserts are less delicious. Try them all.

With desserts, probably more then any other foods, the end product is only as good as the ingredients used. Good quality chocolate, unsalted butter, and cake flour are important ingredients in dessert making.

Use the best quality chocolate you can afford. Chocolate chips are great in cookies and can often be used in fillings, but a good quality, pure chocolate is better for glazes and dipping. Candy stores often sell a good quality, but still affordable, bulk chocolate that will work well for this purpose.

Please use unsalted butter when indicated in the recipe. If just a small amount of butter is used for cooking, I really don't think that it is terribly important to use unsalted butter. In desserts, however, it makes a big difference. Unsalted butter gives a mellow taste and does not add extra salt where it is not needed.

Also, some recipes do need cake flour. I have found that using all purpose flour and just reducing the amount, as sometimes directed, does not give the same results.

It is also important to have ingredients at the temperatures directed in the recipe. If the ingredient is not softened, at room temperature, or chilled as directed, it will affect the finished product. Egg whites whip into higher peaks at room temperature. Cream whips better when chilled. Butter can change the entire texture of a recipe if not at the correct temperature. By the way, when the temperature is not specified in the ingredient list, it is assumed to be at room temperature.

So . . . let's have our cake and eat it too—maybe just a tiny slice.

Hazelnut Caramel Apple Pizza

This recipe was tried out on hundreds of high school home economics students through the Oregon Hazelnut Marketing Board's education program. It generally received an A plus.

1½ cups all purpose white flour

1¾ cup coarsely chopped toasted
    hazelnuts, divided

⅓ cup granulated sugar

¼ teaspoon salt

½ cup plus 1 tablespoon chilled unsalted
    butter, cut into ½-inch pieces

1¼ cup chocolate chips, divided

2 to 3 medium apples, peeled and
    thinly sliced, about 3 cups

3 tablespoons brown sugar

½ teaspoon ground cinnamon

12 cream caramels, unwrapped

1 tablespoon water

Position a baking rack in the center of the oven and heat oven to 350 degrees.

Place flour, one cup of the hazelnuts, sugar, and salt in a food processor work bowl fitted with a metal blade. Process for about 30 seconds or until the hazelnuts are finely chopped.

Add ½ cup butter and process for about 15 seconds or until butter is the size of coarse meal and the mixture just holds together when a small amount is pressed between your fingers. Pulse with one to two teaspoons cold water if the dough does not stick together.

Press the mixture evenly into a 12-inch round pizza pan. Bake in the center of a 350-degree oven for 15 to 18 minutes or until the edges are golden and the center is firm. Do not overbake. Remove from the oven and immediately sprinkle with ¾ cup chocolate chips. Let stand several minutes until melted. Spread melted chocolate evenly over the crust. Let stand at room temperature, or refrigerate until chocolate is firm.

Melt remaining one tablespoon butter in large skillet. Sauté apples until fork-tender. Toss with brown sugar and cinnamon. Cool to room temperature.

Melt remaining chocolate in microwave or double boiler. Place caramels and one tablespoon water in a small microwave-safe bowl. Microwave just until caramels are softened, about 30 to 60 seconds. Stir until smooth.

Spread apples evenly over crust. Sprinkle with remaining chopped hazelnuts. Drizzle with caramel sauce and melted chocolate. Let stand at room temperature until the chocolate is firm, about one hour. Slice with pizza cutter. Serves 8 to 12.

EASE OF
PREPARATION: 2

PREPARATION TIME:
15 MINUTES

BAKING TIME:
15 TO 18 MINUTES

COOLING TIME:
2 HOURS AT ROOM
TEMPERATURE;
1 HOUR
REFRIGERATED

YIELD: 8 SERVINGS

NOTE: The best way to melt the caramels is in the microwave oven. However, they should be checked very carefully, since they burn easily.

White Chocolate-Hazelnut Cheesecake with Raspberry Garnish

🌰 🌰 🌰

EASE OF
PREPARATION: 3

PREPARATION TIME:
45 MINUTES

BAKING TIME:
45 MINUTES,
PLUS 1 HOUR
COOLING IN OVEN

SPECIAL
EQUIPMENT:
WELL-GREASED
9-INCH SPRING
FORM PAN

YIELD:
12 SERVINGS

FOR PHOTO:
SEE PAGE 112

This creamy, smooth cheesecake tastes as good as it looks. It is well worth the extra time to frost it with the White Chocolate Cream Cheese Frosting, although it is also delicious served plain with just a bit of Raspberry Sauce on the side.

To keep the top from cracking as it cools, be sure to grease the pan well and to cool away from drafts.

Hazelnut Crust

25 vanilla wafers (1 cup crushed)
1 tablespoon granulated sugar
½ cup coarsely chopped toasted hazelnuts
2 tablespoons melted unsalted butter

🌰

Generously butter a nine-inch spring form pan. Cover the outside of the pan and up the sides about two inches with wide aluminum foil. This will prevent water from seeping in the pan while baking.

In a food processor, finely chop vanilla wafers. Add sugar and hazelnuts; chop fine. With the machine running, pour in butter. Press the mixture into the bottom of the prepared pan. Refrigerate until firm.

The Cheesecake

3 ounces white chocolate, chopped
⅓ cup whipping cream
¾ cup granulated sugar
3 strips lemon peel, cut in ½ inch pieces
1½ pounds cream cheese, softened
1 cup sour cream
2 tablespoons fresh lemon juice
4 large eggs
• Raspberry Grand-Marnier Sauce
• White Chocolate/Cream Cheese Frosting
1 cup medium chopped toasted hazelnuts
• Fresh raspberries

🌰

Position a baking rack in the center of the oven and heat oven to 350 degrees.

Place white chocolate in small bowl. Gently warm cream and pour over the chocolate. Let stand, stirring often, until chocolate is melted. Cool slightly.

Place sugar and lemon peel in a food processor work bowl fitted with a metal blade. Process until the lemon peel is very fine, about one minute. Add softened cream cheese and process until smooth, about 30 seconds, scraping the sides of the bowl several times. Mix in white chocolate, cream, sour cream, and lemon juice. Add eggs, one at a time, and process until smooth, another 30 seconds. Pour half of the mixture over the chilled crust, and drizzle with ¼ cup of the Raspberry Sauce. Top with remaining batter.

Place the cheesecake in a baking pan about 2½ to 3 inches deep and wide enough so there is at least an inch of room around the cheesecake. Pour boiling water into the baking pan to about half way up the sides of the spring form pan.

Bake in the center of a 350-degree oven for 45 minutes. Turn oven off and let cheesecake remain in oven, with door closed, for another 60 minutes. Remove from waterbath and cool in the pan, away from drafts. When cool, remove from pan and refrigerate.

To finish dessert, cut a piece of parchment or waxed paper in a six-inch round, using a saucer as a guide, and place in the center of the cheesecake. Frost the sides and top, around the paper, with White Chocolate & Cream Cheese Frosting. Press chopped hazelnuts into the frosting. Remove paper and chill until frosting is firm, about one hour. Spoon Raspberry Grand-Marnier Sauce into the center and garnish with fresh raspberries.

White Chocolate Frosting

2 tablespoons whipping cream
2 ounces white chocolate, chopped
4 ounces cream cheese, softened
1 teaspoon lemon zest
    (See Glossary, page 123-124)

❦

Place whipping cream in a small bowl and gently heat. Add white chocolate to cream and stir until melted. Cool to room temperature.

With electric mixer beat cream cheese and lemon zest together. Add white chocolate and cream; whip until smooth. If frosting is too soft, refrigerate until it is slightly chilled and then whip until it is thick and creamy.

Raspberry-Grand Marnier Sauce

16 ounces fresh or frozen raspberries
    (1 cup juice)
⅓ to ¾ cup granulated sugar, or to taste
2 tablespoons orange liqueur
    (such as Grand Marnier)

❦

In a saucepan, heat berries until just warm, and juice is released. If using fresh berries, add ¼ cup water. Force the mixture through a sieve or juicer. Return juice to saucepan; discard solids. Add sugar to taste. If using fresh berries ⅓ to ½ cup sugar should be adequate. If using pre-sweetened berries, little or no additional sugar may be needed. Cook over medium high heat until liquid is reduced by half. Remove from heat, add orange liqueur and cool.

NOTE: White confectionery products with cocoa butter as an ingredient are generally referred to as white chocolate. The term "white chocolate" is a misnomer, however, as chocolate refers to the brown chocolate liqueur found when processing the cocoa beans. Look for cocoa butter listed as the first ingredient on the package, as the higher the ratio of cocoa butter in the product, the finer the confection. If cocoa butter is not listed as an ingredient, the product is a white compound or confectioner's coating. White chocolate should be handled carefully. It should not be overheated. In this recipe, the cream should be just barely warm enough to gently melt the chocolate. If the chocolate gets too warm, it may "seize" and refuse to melt.

DID YOU KNOW . . . That hazelnut trees are known for their longevity. There are a number of orchards in Oregon that are over a half-century old and still producing good crops.

Poached Pears with Hazelnut Ganache & Fresh Raspberry Sauce

EASE OF
PREPARATION: 2

PREPARATION TIME:
20 MINUTES

COOKING TIME:
10 TO 15 MINUTES

CHILLING TIME:
1 TO 2 HOURS

YIELD: 4 OR 8
SERVINGS

TIP: In order for the pear to stand up right, cut a small slice off the bottom of the pear before filling with Ganache.

NOTE: If a smaller portion is desired, cut the pears in half and fill the cavity with the Chocolate Ganache. To serve, place chocolate side down in sauce. Makes 8 smaller servings.

NOTE: The leftover poaching liquid can be frozen and used as a base for fruit soups or sorbets.

This is such a simple, yet elegant dessert. Because pears are available all year round, it can be served for the holidays, as well as during summer months when berries are in season.

4 fresh, ripe pears
    (Bartlett, Comice, Anjou)
¼ cup, plus 1 tablespoon, lemon juice
3 cups water
1 cup granulated sugar
1 cinnamon stick
6 whole cloves
• Chocolate Hazelnut Ganache
• Raspberry Grand-Marnier Sauce
    (See Page 115)
• Chocolate leaves and stems for garnish

Peel pears and remove cores with an apple/pear corer, leaving the stem end intact; rub with fresh lemon juice. In a two-quart saucepan, bring water, sugar, cinnamon, and cloves to boil. Add ¼ cup lemon juice and reduce heat to simmer. Poach pears, adding water to cover if necessary, until they are slightly softened. Time varies, depending upon the ripeness of the pear, but usually several minutes is enough.

Remove pears from poaching liquid. Rapidly chill the liquid by placing pan in a sink of ice water. Return pears to chilled liquid, making sure that they are completely covered, and refrigerate until ready to use, up to 12 hours.

To serve, remove pears from liquid, pat off excess moisture and fill centers with several tablespoons of the Chocolate Hazelnut Ganache. Garnish with chocolate leaf and, if desired, remove natural stem and replace with chocolate stem. Serve on a pool of Raspberry Grand-Marnier Sauce.

Chocolate Hazelnut Ganache
¼ cup heavy cream
4 ounces semisweet chocolate,
    finely chopped
¼ cup finely ground toasted hazelnuts

Heat cream and pour over chopped chocolate. Stir until chocolate is melted and shiny. Stir in hazelnuts. Let stand at room temperature until slightly thickened.

Chocolate Leaves & Stems
Melt confectioners' coating chocolate (see Intro to Candy, page 105) to 82 degrees. With small brush or knife spread chocolate on the underside (veined side) of several small, nontoxic leaves (I use rose leaves from my garden that I know have not been treated with chemicals), taking care not to get any of the chocolate on the top side, or it will be difficult to remove the leaf. Refrigerate until firm, about ten minutes. Gently pull the leaf away from the chocolate. Make several extras in case there is breakage.

For the stems, pour several tablespoons of chocolate on a baking sheet. Let stand until it is almost firm, but is still pliable. With a pastry scraper, scrape under the chocolate, letting it roll into a small pencil. With fingers form into a stem. Cut to desired size.

Chocolate Hazelnut Cream

This dessert is so good, it's hard to believe that it is so simple. It can also be made a day in advance.

¾ cup, plus 1 tablespoon, whipping cream
3 egg yolks
8 ounces milk chocolate, chopped
¼ cup unsalted butter
¼ cup coffee-flavored liqueur
   (such as Kahlua)
1 ounce semisweet chocolate, chopped
¼ cup medium chopped toasted hazelnuts

Place ¾ cup cream in saucepan and heat to lukewarm. Whisk in egg yolks, one at time, and heat to 160 degrees, stirring constantly. (See Eggs, Glossary, pages 123-124). Have a larger pan of ice water nearby and place the bottom of the pan in the ice water to immediately stop cooking.

Remove from heat and stir in milk chocolate and butter until melted. Stir in liqueur. In microwave, or top half of double boiler, melt semisweet chocolate. Remove about one cup of the milk chocolate mixture to a small bowl and stir in semisweet chocolate and the remaining one tablespoon of cream.

Refrigerate milk chocolate mixture until it is of pouring consistency. Because of the small amount of the semisweet chocolate, it may stand at room temperature while the milk chocolate is chilling. If the semisweet chocolate gets too firm, heat slightly to bring to pouring consistency.

To serve, place about one tablespoon of the dark chocolate mixture in the bottom of each of six champagne glasses or sherbets. With a spoon, swirl the chocolate around, about half way up the glass. Sprinkle with chopped hazelnuts. Divide milk chocolate mixture among the six glasses. Top with a swirl of the remaining dark chocolate. Refrigerate until chilled, about two hours. Garnish with a fresh strawberry if strawberries are in season.

EASE OF PREPARATION: 1

PREPARATION TIME: 20 MINUTES

CHILL TIME: 2 HOURS

YIELD: 6 SERVINGS

NOTE: A mint or hazelnut-flavored liqueur may be substituted for the coffee liqueur.

Chocolate Raspberry Truffle Torte

○ ○ ○ ○

EASE OF
PREPARATION: 4

PREPARATION TIME:
40 MINUTES

BAKING TIME:
25 MINUTES

CHILLING TIME:
1 HOUR

SPECIAL
EQUIPMENT: 9 INCH
SPRING FORM PAN

YIELD: 12 SERVINGS

FOR PHOTO:
SEE PAGE 4

NOTE: Because the
egg foam is the only
form of leavening in
this recipe, it should
be handled carefully
so the air bubbles do
not deflate. Gently,
but thoroughly, first
fold the dry
ingredients, and then
the butter mixture
into the egg foam.

This light, airy cake makes a perfect backdrop for the dense chocolate truffle filling.

½ cup sifted cake flour
¼ cup Dutch process cocoa
　　(See Glossary, pages 123-124)
4 large eggs, room temperature
½ cup granulated sugar
2 tablespoons butter

○

Position a baking rack in the center of the oven and heat oven to 350 degrees. Cut a nine-inch round of parchment paper and place in bottom of a nine-inch spring form pan. Grease and flour lightly. Tap out excess flour.

In a small bowl, sift cocoa and cake flour together. Reserve.

Place eggs and sugar in a large mixing bowl and beat with an electric mixer until they triple in volume and are light, lemon colored, and the texture of soft whipped cream. (The eggs have been beaten long enough when the batter falls from the beaters in ribbons and lies on top of the bowl without sinking). This should take about eight minutes in a standing mixer or ten minutes with a hand mixer.

In the meantime, in a small bowl soften butter until it is just barely melted.

Sift the cocoa/flour mixture over the eggs in three or four additions; gently fold in with a whisk or rubber spatula. Remove about ½ cup of the batter and gently fold into the butter. Gently fold the butter mixture into the batter. Carefully pour batter into prepared pan.

Bake in the center of a 350-degree oven for about 25 to 28 minutes or just until it starts to pull away from the side of the pan, and a wooden pick inserted into the center comes out clean. Cool for ten minutes on a rack; then remove the outer ring. When cool, remove the bottom.

Slice the cooled cake in half and spread one side to within ½ inch of the edges with about ⅓ cup of the Raspberry Sauce; spread the other half with the Chocolate Truffle Filling. Put the two layers together. Frost with a very thin base coat of the Chocolate Glaze.

Refrigerate until firm. Soften remaining glaze to pouring consistency, and pour in the center of the cake. Tilt the cake so the glaze runs down the sides, spreading with a knife only if necessary. Let stand until firm.

Truffle Filling

⅓ cup whipping cream
1 egg yolk
6 ounces semisweet chocolate
⅓ cup medium chopped toasted hazelnuts*

In a small saucepan over medium heat, whisk egg yolk into cream, stirring constantly until the temperature reaches 160 degrees. (See Eggs, Glossary, pages 123-124) Immediately remove from heat and stir in chocolate until it is melted. Fold in hazelnuts. Cool to spreading consistency.

* NOTE: Crunchy hazelnut butter may be used in place of the chopped toasted hazelnuts.

Chocolate Glaze

6 ounces semisweet chocolate
¼ cup unsalted butter
¼ cup whipping cream

In a microwave or the top half of a double boiler, heat chocolate, butter, and cream. Stir until smooth. Let glaze stand until slightly thickened, but still easily poured.

Raspberry Sauce

16 ounces fresh or frozen raspberries
    (1 cup juice)
⅓ to ½ cup granulated sugar*
1 tablespoon cornstarch

In a saucepan, heat berries until just warm and juice is released. Force mixture through sieve or juicer. Return juice to the saucepan, reserving two tablespoons in a small cup; discard solids.

*Add sugar to taste. If you are using presweetened berries, little or no additional sugar may be needed. Cook over medium high heat until liquid is reduced by a third. Stir cornstarch into the reserved raspberry juice. Whisk into the sauce and stir until thickened.

PRESENTATION TIP: Serve in a pool of Raspberry Sauce. To make the chocolate heart design in the raspberry sauce, soften a little of the Chocolate Glaze. Pipe three circles on top of the raspberry sauce and pull a knife through the center, making a heart design.

NOTE: Snip a tiny tip off the corner of small plastic bag to make an instant cake decorating bag.

Fresh Pear & Hazelnut Kuchen

EASE OF
PREPARATION: 2

PREPARATION TIME:
10 MINUTES

BAKING TIME:
25 TO 30 MINUTES

SPECIAL
EQUIPMENT:
10 TO 12 INCH TART
PAN WITH
REMOVABLE RING

YIELD: 1 PASTRY,
8 SERVINGS

NOTE: An easy way to remove the ring from a tart pan is to loosen the pastry with the tip of a knife and set the center of the pan on a glass. Just let the ring fall to the counter. To remove the bottom, slide a long metal spatula or fillet knife between the pastry and the pan to loosen; slide off onto a serving plate.

An excellent way to top off this simple tart is with sweetened whipped cream lightly dusted with fresh nutmeg or a sprinkle of shaved white chocolate.

3 ripe, fresh pears
    (Bartlett, Comice, Anjou)
• Fresh lemon juice
1 cup all purpose white flour
⅓ cup granulated white sugar
1 teaspoon baking powder
¼ teaspoon baking soda
1 cup coarsely chopped toasted hazelnuts
5 tablespoons cold unsalted butter,
    cut into ½ inch pieces
1 large egg
¼ cup sour cream
2 tablespoons brown sugar

Position a baking rack in the center of the oven and heat oven to 375 degrees.

Peel and core pears, rub with fresh lemon juice, and set aside.

In a food processor work bowl fitted with a metal blade, place flour, sugar, baking powder, baking soda, and ½ cup toasted hazelnuts. Process until nuts are finely chopped, about 30 seconds. Add butter and process until it is like a coarse meal.

Whisk egg and sour cream together and pour over flour mixture. Process just until ingredients are evenly moistened, about ten seconds.

Spray a tart pan with nonstick vegetable spray. Spoon batter into pan and, with moistened finger tips, spread evenly over the bottom and about ½ inch up the sides.

Slice pears into ¼ inch slices. Spread slices on top of the batter to form an overlapping circle, reserving enough slices to also cover the batter in the center. Squeeze lemon juice over the pears, and sprinkle with brown sugar and the remaining coarsely chopped hazelnuts.

Bake in the center of a preheated 375-degree oven until puffed and golden, about 25 to 30 minutes. Let cool for about five minutes and, with the tip of a knife, release the pastry from the ring. Remove ring and cool. The bottom of the pan can be removed when cool, but it is not necessary.

Serve slightly warm or at room temperature with vanilla ice cream or whipped cream.

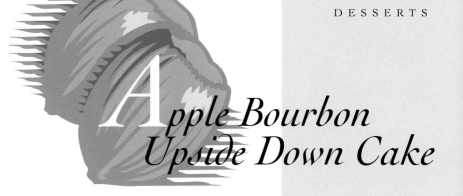

Apple Bourbon Upside Down Cake

To save on dish washing, an oven-safe, heavy skillet works well for this recipe. The cake will keep overnight at room temperature. Reheat in microwave.

Apple-Bourbon Topping

6 tablespoons unsalted butter, divided
2 medium tart, ripe apples, peeled, cored, and sliced in thin rings
  (use Rome Beauty, Granny Smith, etc.)
½ cup brown sugar
2 tablespoons bourbon
½ teaspoon ground cinnamon
¼ cup medium chopped toasted hazelnuts

Melt one tablespoon butter in a ten-inch skillet. Sauté half the apple rings for several minutes or just until they start to color. Carefully remove to a large plate; reserve. Repeat with another tablespoon of butter and sauté the remaining apples.

Melt remaining butter in skillet. Mix in brown sugar and cook, over high heat, for about one minute until sugar dissolves. Add the bourbon and cook for another minute. Remove from the heat. Cool to room temperature and arrange apple slices in the sauce, over-lapping one another, in a ring about one inch from the edge of the pan. Sprinkle with cinnamon. Spoon hazelnuts in the center of the ring and around the edges. Prepare cake batter.

Upside Down Cake

1½ cups sifted cake flour
1 teaspoon baking powder
¼ teaspoon baking soda
¼ teaspoon ground cinnamon
½ teaspoon salt
¾ cup granulated sugar
1 stick (½ cup butter), softened
2 large eggs
½ cup buttermilk
1 teaspoon vanilla

Position a baking rack in the center of the oven and heat oven to 350 degrees.

In a small bowl, whisk together cake flour, baking powder, baking soda, cinnamon, and salt. Reserve.

In a two or three quart mixing bowl, with electric mixer, beat sugar and butter together until smooth. Add eggs; beat until well mixed. Alternately mix in buttermilk and reserved dry ingredients and beat until smooth, about one minute. Mix in vanilla.

Pour batter evenly over the topping, spreading smooth with a knife. Bake in the center of a 350-degree oven for about 35 minutes, or until top is golden and a wooden pick inserted in the center comes out clean.

Remove from oven, let stand for several minutes, and loosen edges with a knife. Invert on a serving plate, and let stand for about a minute before removing skillet so that all the topping is loosened. Serve warm with whipped cream flavored with a little sugar and bourbon.

EASE OF
PREPARATION: 2

PREPARATION TIME:
20 MINUTES

BAKING TIME:
30 TO 35 MINUTES

YIELD:
6 TO 8 SERVINGS

NOTE: The bourbon can be omitted if desired. Instead, substitute two teaspoons vanilla.

Chocolate, Coconut, & Hazelnut Bread Pudding

Some of the old desserts are still the best. Teamed with chocolate and coconut, this up-dated version of Grandmother's bread pudding is in style again. It can be made a day in advance and reheated before serving.

1 cup light cream (Half & Half)
¼ cup Dutch process cocoa
    (See Glossary, pages 123-124)
3 large eggs
2 egg yolks
1 cup sugar
 3 cups milk
¼ cup hazelnut liqueur
    (such as Frangelico)
8 cups cubed dry French bread
    (about 8 ounces)
1 cup flaked coconut
½ cup coarsely chopped, toasted hazelnuts

Position a baking rack in the center of the oven and heat oven to 350 degrees.

Lightly spray a two-quart, shallow baking dish with nonstick vegetable spray.

In the microwave or in a saucepan, heat cream until simmering. Add cocoa and stir until it is dissolved. Set aside.

In a two-quart bowl, whisk eggs and egg yolks until well mixed. Whisk in sugar, milk and hazelnut liqueur. Stir in reserved cocoa mixture.

Spread half of the bread cubes in prepared pan. Pour half of the liquid over the bread. Sprinkle with half of the coconut and hazelnuts. Add remaining bread and liquid and top with remaining coconut and hazelnuts.

Bake in the center of a 350-degree oven for about one hour until a knife inserted into the center comes out clean.

Serve at room temperature, or slightly warm with sweetened whipped cream or with an added dash of hazelnut liqueur, if desired.

Glossary

Bread Crumbs are used in several forms—fresh, dried, and toasted. To make bread crumbs, place torn pieces of bread (for most purposes, the crusts may be included) in food processor and chop until fine. For toasted bread crumbs, melt 1 tablespoon butter in a large skillet, add up to 4 cups fresh bread crumbs, and toss with butter. Stir often over low heat, cooking until crumbs are dried and golden, about 20 minutes. All types may be frozen.

Butter, Salted is used for most everyday table purposes. It can also be used in recipes where a little additional salt will not noticeably affect the flavor.

Butter, Unsalted should be used in fine pastries and confections and in delicately flavored sauces where additional salt would be undesirable.

Butter, Clarified, also known as drawn butter, is used when a pure clear fat is preferred, such as in Phyllo pastries, where salt and milk solids in the butter will discolor pastry when baking. An easy way to clarify butter is to melt the butter, then refrigerate it until solid. The milk solids and moisture sink to the bottom and can easily be scraped away with a knife and discarded. The remaining is clarified butter.

Capers are buds of a plant that grows in the Mediterranean area. They are pickled in a vinegar brine and are used in salads and sauces where their unique flavor is desired. Generally, smaller capers have a better flavor than the large.

Cocoa, (Dutch process) has been treated with an alkali to neutralize the cocoa's natural acidity. It is generally darker and more intense in flavor than regular cocoa.

Deglazing the pan means adding liquid to a hot pan to release particles left in the pan from cooking meat, poultry, or fish. This mixture is the flavor base for many sauces.

Eggs—Unless otherwise indicated, all recipes call for large eggs. Although the occurrence of salmonella bacteria in raw eggs has been very small, much attention has been focused on proper cooking techniques and temperatures. As improper handling techniques were associated with nearly all reported cases of food poisoning associated with eggs, it is important that eggs be clean, fresh, and stored in the refrigerator. To eliminate possible contamination, eggs must

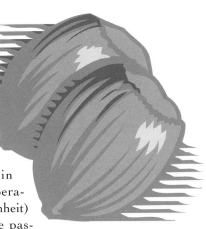

be heated to prescribed temperatures. This is generally not a problem in baking or in cooking when the internal temperature is over 160° Fahrenheit; however, when eggs are used in uncooked or low temperature (under 160° Fahrenheit) recipes, they should be pasteurized before using. Currently, the American Egg Board recommends two methods of pasteurizing eggs: In one method, eggs are mixed with liquid (2 tablespoons liquid to 1 raw egg), cooked to 140 degrees Fahrenheit and held at that temperature for 3½ minutes. The other method is to mix eggs with liquid, and cook to an endpoint of 160°. (See American Eggboard publication, *Salmonella & Egg Safety*.)

Fillo/Phyllo Dough is the tissue-thin Greek or Eastern dough that is used to create many delicate layers of pastry in Tiropetes, Spanokopita, and Baklava. See page 15 for information on how to use this dough.

Flour, All purpose, a mixture of hard and soft wheats, can be used for most general purposes. It comes bleached and unbleached. Unbleached flour has a slightly higher gluten or protein count than bleached.

Flour, Bread is a blend of hard wheats designed especially for bread making. It has a very high gluten content, which improves elasticity and generally makes a better loaf than all purpose flours.

Flour, Cake is a blend of soft wheat flours, which makes it ideal for delicate cakes and pastries.

Flour, Whole Wheat is a high fiber, nutritious flour that contains the wheat germ. Because whole grain flours produce a heavy loaf, they are generally used along with white flours to help lighten the product.

Hazelnut Butter is similar to peanut butter, but with a rich toasted flavor. Because of the fine texture, it is difficult to make in the home kitchen.

Hazelnut Paste can be made in the food processor by grinding toasted hazelnuts just until finely chopped, but stopping before the oil is released, as in butter. By adding sugar and flavorings, such as extracts and liqueurs, the paste can be used as fillings for cakes, candies, and truffles.

Herbs, Dried—Because dried herbs are so much more concentrated than fresh, the general rule is to use only half the amount when using dried. This does not always apply, however, especially with more pungent herbs like rosemary, oregano, and thyme, when a little less may be better.

Herbs, Fresh—While most recipes in this book give an amount for using both fresh and dried herbs, fresh herbs are almost always preferred for their unique flavor and aroma. Most supermarkets carry some of the more common culinary fresh herbs, but a kitchen garden assures a continual supply. Whether grown in a pot on the patio or as part of the landscape, herb gardening offers the convenience of a snip or two just steps away. Chives, parsley, basil, dill, oregano, thyme, tarragon, rosemary, mint, and sage are the foundation of an herb garden. Cilantro, chervil, borage, hyssop, lemon balm, lovage, sorrel, and savory, are nice additions as space permits.

Margarine can often be substituted for butter when cooking. However, baking is a little more tricky. Texture and browning ability may be affected if margarine is subtituted in some pies, cakes, and confections. Also, many low-fat whipped margarines contain added moisture which then adds moisture instead of fat to the product.

Microwave cooking times are not given because of the wide variation in wattage of microwave ovens. Please refer to the oven handbook for precise times for your oven.

Oil, Hazelnut is pressed from hazelnuts and has a very prominent hazelnut flavor. It is especially good drizzled on vegetables and in salad dressings. At one time, most of the hazelnut oil was imported, but now it is being produced by Oregon manufacturers.

Oil, Olive is available in several forms and colors. Extra Virgin Olive Oil, from the first pressing of the olives, is generally the best quality. Like wine, olive oil should be purchased to please the individual palate. Some are very fruity and flavorful; others are somewhat bland. The newer "light" olive oils are light in flavor and color, but not in calories.

Oil, Vegetable is often used when a light, clear non-flavored oil is specified. Canola, safflower, corn, and soybean oil are all recommended when a light-tasting oil is needed.

Parmesan, the delicious hard, dry cheese, was once available only in little green boxes, but now cheese shops carry many varieties, both domestic and imported. The standard to meet for parmesan cheese is that of Italy's **Parmiggiano Reggiano.** This robust, yet mellow, cheese is generally a little more expensive than the others, but may

actually be more economical overall because with its intense flavor, less is needed.

Reduce/Reduction intensifies the flavor, usually in a sauce and stock, by boiling the liquid down until desired strength is reached.

Shallots, which are grown in cloves like garlic, have a mild onion flavor. In spring the tender shoots can be eaten like green onions. The mature bulbs are used in delicate sauces when just a hint of onion is desired.

Sundried Tomatoes are available both dried or oil packed. If using the oil packed, place the tomatoes between several thicknesses of paper towels to absorb the excess oil. Sometimes the dry pack can be very hard and dry. If this is the case, reconstitute by soaking in a little olive oil and chopped garlic. Again, pat off the excess oil prior to using.

Tomatoes only deserve the name when they are vine ripened. Hot house tomatoes should be called something else because they seem to be an entirely different species. When vine ripened tomatoes are unavailable, try using firm, red Romas, which have a good texture and are good keepers. If neither of the above are available, use a good brand of canned tomatoes, especially when making salsa and sauces.

Yeast—Baking yeast is available in two forms, moist cakes and in dry granular form, which is most often used by home cooks. The granular form is avilable in $\frac{1}{4}$-ounce individual packages as well as in bulk. Consumers can choose between the regular yeast and the instant, or quick rise yeast, which will activate about 50% faster than the former under proper temperatures. Because yeast is a living organism, care should be taken to keep it fresh and alive. It should be stored in a cool, dry place, as high temperatures can damage the yeast. Store in refrigerator or freezer.

Zest—Citrus zest, lemon or orange, is an important ingredient in many of the recipes in this book. The zest is the very thin outer layer of peel of the citrus which contains the oil and the sweet, intense flavor of the citrus. For small amounts, zest can be removed with a tool called a zester. For larger jobs, a potato peeler works well to remove very thin strips of peel. Try not to remove any of the bitter white pith, however. The thin strips can be finely chopped with a sharp chef's knife. When sugar is a part of the recipe, the food processor can do much of the work. Place about 1 cup sugar in the work bowl fitted with the metal blade. Add up to 2 tablespoons peel, cut into $\frac{1}{2}$-inch pieces and process until the peel is very fine, about two minutes. This mixture can also be dried and used as flavored sugar.

Index